THE LAST DITCH

Eamonn Sweeney writes the Hold The Back Page column for the *Sunday Independent* and a Monday sports column for the *Irish Independent*. He is a former Irish Sports Columnist of the Year and has written seven books, including the novels *Waiting for the Healer* and *The Photograph* and the sports books *There's Only One Red Army* and *The Road to Croker*.

Born in Sligo in 1968, he lives in Skibbereen and is the father of three daughters. He is the owner of a dog and a bearded dragon and headed three goals during his otherwise undistinguished under-age Gaelic football career. All the other personal stuff is in the book.

The Last Ditch

HOW ONE GAA CHAMPIONSHIP GAVE A SPORTSWRITER BACK HIS LIFE

EAMONN SWEENEY

HACHETTE
BOOKS
IRELAND

First published in Ireland in 2025 by HACHETTE BOOKS IRELAND

1

Cataloguing in Publication Data is available from the British Library

Trade paperback ISBN 9781399734639
Ebook ISBN 9781399734646

Typeset in Berling Antiqua by Bookends Publishing Services, Dublin
Printed and bound in Great Britain by Clays Ltd, Elcograf S.p.A.

Hachette Books Ireland policy is to use papers that are natural, renewable
and recyclable products and made from wood grown in sustainable forests.
The logging and manufacturing processes are expected to conform to the
environmental regulations of the country of origin.

MIX
Paper | Supporting
responsible forestry
FSC
www.fsc.org
FSC® C104740

Hachette Books Ireland
8 Castlecourt Centre
Castleknock
Dublin 15, Ireland

A division of Hachette UK Ltd
Carmelite House, 50 Victoria Embankment, London EC4Y 0DZ

www.hachettebooksireland.ie

Contents

To my daughters Emily, Isabel and Lara

Prologue

High Noon in Ardrahan

8 January 2024

I WAS IN ARDRAHAN TWO WEEKS AFTER CHRISTMAS. No one else was. I'd taken a bus here only to discover there didn't seem to be any actual 'here'. There was a closed pub, a few houses with no visible sign of life and no one on the street. I waited a bit. Still nothing. Not even noise. Maybe nuclear war had been declared while I was on the bus.

In desperation, I waved down a passing car. The driver looked at me with alarm and kept going. A man on a tractor proved equally unobliging.

Eventually I met a woman out walking and asked her where the railway station was. The village signpost seemed ambiguous about its location. She said it was about three-quarters of a mile away. A cutting wind accompanied me out a country road with no footpath. It was an unlikely route to a railway station.

Yet there it was down a lane to my right. The station had the same kind of barely there air as the village. There was a small shelter, a ticket machine and one set of rails. It was the kind of halt where gunslingers wait for trains while a rusty weathervane creaks in the breeze and vultures perch hopefully overhead.

A few boisterous teenagers turned up to join me on the platform. The sight of the approaching train made my heart pound. It lumbered to a stop in front of me. If I could sit on my own I might be OK. I stepped on, feeling a familiar vertiginous sensation as I did so. The teenagers got on and sat right across from me. The doors shut with a whoosh. The trap was closed.

It was *High Noon* in Ardrahan. If I stayed on the train my life would change. If I didn't, I would trek back into the village, contact the editor of this book and tell her I couldn't write it. The fears that had imprisoned me for decades would win yet again.

There was still time to press the button, open the door and step back on the platform. It would only take a moment.

1

On the Road Again?

Three months earlier

WHEN THE PUBLISHERS ASKED ME TO WRITE THIS book in October 2023, I knew two things. The first was that I really wanted to, the second was that I wouldn't be able.

They wanted a sequel to my 2004 book *The Road to Croker*, which followed the 2003 GAA championships. It seemed an interesting idea. So much had changed in the intervening years. The country had changed, the championship had changed and I'd changed.

Back in 2003, Simon Harris was doing his Leaving Cert and Leo Varadkar his college medical exams. In the previous year's general election, Fianna Fáil had won eighty-one seats, fifty more than their nearest challenger. Sinn Féin won five, three less than the Progressive Democrats. Those days are gone forever.

In 2003, I could say the GAA was part of who we are and what brings us together. Twenty years on, I was less sure of what 'we' meant, or who belonged to 'us', or even if it was a good idea to use those terms anymore.

In 2003, September was synonymous with All-Ireland finals. That year, the championships began on 4 May and ended on 28 September. But in 2018 the hurling decider was switched to August and in 2021 both finals switched to July. The 2024 championships were scheduled to run from 6 April to 28 July.

The change was due to Covid-19 doing the unthinkable in 2020 by halting all GAA activity. When action resumed after a four-month break the association opted to play club competitions first. The inter-county championships didn't begin till November, took place in empty stadiums and finished just six days before Christmas.

GAA top brass liked the 'split season' so much they decided to make it permanent. From August onwards it's club games only. It feels a bit unnatural.

Championship structures had changed too. Hurling now had an immensely exciting round-robin format in Munster with five evenly matched teams engaging in a cut-throat battle for three qualifying places.

Football was now saddled with an impossibly convoluted structure where twenty-four games are played in the qualifier group stages merely to knock out four teams in the top tier. The two-tier system was new as well.

If you'd asked fans in 2003 to pick the GAA's two biggest underachievers, Dublin footballers and Limerick hurlers would have come out on top. The Dubs were knocked out of Leinster by Laois that year. Limerick departed after a loss to Offaly in the qualifiers.

Both teams would begin 2024 as All-Ireland champions. It was a familiar feeling. Dublin had won six in a row from 2015 to 2020 and recaptured their title after a two-year break. Limerick were going for a record-breaking five in a row.

The championship landscape wasn't the only thing looking radically different these days. I was thirty-five when I wrote *The Road to Croker*. My eldest daughter was just a year old. Shortly after I'd finished writing it, my father died of cancer. I'd changed from being his son to being someone's father.

By 2023, I had three daughters and being their father was the greatest thing that had ever happened to me. By the time the 2024 championship began, my eldest would be doing her final college exams, one of the twins would be facing her Leaving Cert and the other would also be leaving the school system. Soon I'd be spending less time with my children. The excitement I felt about seeing them embark on their futures was tinged with a certain sadness.

There was a lot of drinking in the first book. Now I'd been off the drink for five years and the chance to hit the championship trail again sober appealed to me. Drinkers are notoriously fond of constructing a carapace to protect them from the scrutiny of not just others but themselves. Sober, there'd be no hiding place. This book would be written by a person rather than a persona.

It'd also be written by a fifty-six-year-old, someone who looks in the mirror and wonders where the old guy came from. I was just three years younger than both my father and my grandfather were when they died. My steps weren't exactly being dogged by a guy with a scythe who fancied a game of chess but I'd greet my sixtieth birthday with a certain relief all the same. This oldest swinger in town might pop an extra blood pressure tablet to celebrate.

Getting on inclines you towards nostalgia, perhaps because you've got a lot more past than future to be thinking about. Memories pull you up short at unexpected moments. You spend time trying to recapture the texture of old days which suddenly seem like they might hold the key to something important. You remember the places you went to, the people you knew, the songs you listened to, the games you watched. So there was something undeniably attractive about retracing my steps and seeing what memories that might evoke. It would be a trip into the GAA's present and my own past. A kind of personal road movie. I've always loved road movies.

The trade I'd followed for almost forty years seemed to be going the way of the thatcher, the cooper and the lighthouse keeper. Digital media's ability to hoover up advertising revenue had banjaxed the newspaper sector. Seventeen Irish local papers had bitten the dust in the previous decade and a half, two of which, the *Roscommon Champion* and the *Longford News*, I'd once worked for. Being a journalist reminded me of Philip Larkin (the English poet not the Kilkenny hurler) saying that old age was like fighting in the Battle of the Somme as people bit the dust on every side of you. Another round of cutbacks was in the offing at my employer, Independent News and Media. A sense of days being numbered was general across the newspaper industry. This was *Last of the Mohicans* territory. It seemed a good time to get back on the road while I had a job, just in case.

A sense of endings assailed me. My mother, who'd recently turned eighty-five, had suffered a stroke during Covid. She'd made a terrific recovery, as she'd done from breast cancer a decade before, but the possibility of there being a day when she wasn't around loomed ever larger. She was the person who'd taken me to Croke Park for the first time, who'd brought one of my daughters to her first Connacht final, who'd watched matches with me in Clones and Clonakilty, Tuam and Thurles, Butlersbridge and Ballymote and a lot of other non-alliterative venues besides. That felt worth writing about too. While she was still able to read it.

There were all these good reasons to write the book. But one good reason not to outweighed them all. It was also my biggest secret.

2

Panic on the Streets of Killarney

THERE ARE DIFFERENT KINDS OF PANIC ATTACKS.
The classic sweating, heart-racing variety is the one most
people think of. First time you get it you may be convinced
you're having a heart attack. The symptoms are those you see
in a movie, when a harassed businessman clutches at his chest
before being felled by a dodgy ticker. You don't necessarily have
to suffer from long-term anxiety to experience this; a prolonged
bout of drinking or even a particularly stressful day can bring
it on.

Then there's another type. An enormous wave of dread
suddenly crashes over you. There's a cold feeling in the pit of
your stomach. The sensation is overwhelming. You can't really
explain what you're afraid of – it's as though the world is almost
entirely composed of fear.

I'd known both for almost a quarter century. In the match between us, panic was twenty points up at this stage. Anxiety had done to me what Dublin usually did to Kildare.

It all began in Killarney at the Munster football championship semi-final between Kerry and Cork. It was 18 June 2000 and I'd no inkling of what was about to hit me. I'd just published a second novel, I'd been living in west Cork for two years, I was covering GAA for the *Irish Examiner* and a few days earlier I'd done an interview with Dara Ó Cinnéide, who spent more time talking about his (excellent) taste in foreign films than about the upcoming match. The young fella I was then had the bumptious bulletproof confidence of a soldier worried the First World War will be over before he gets there and wins a few medals.

Two days before the game I was on the way to Cork to give a reading of my novel. Coming into Bandon I began to feel odd. It was as if something was weighing down on me. I suddenly felt immensely tired and heard myself saying, 'I can't go on.' I had time before the reading and decided to check out a local doctor just to be on the safe side. He told me I seemed in good physical nick. I asked if there was anything he could do to make sure the feeling didn't return before the reading and he gave me a few Xanax. I'd never heard of them before but felt back to normal shortly after I'd popped one. The reading went well and by the time I was home the Bandon incident already seemed unimportant.

Two days later I went to Killarney. On the way I passed the Cork team, managed at the time by Larry Tompkins, sitting outside a pub on the edge of Ballyvourney in their tracksuits.

It was an ideal afternoon for a match and my biggest worry was whether a couple of Cork players rumoured to be injured would actually start. I went into the ground and was about to walk around to the press box on the other side of the pitch when it hit me. They say you never forget your first time and I remember that first panic attack vividly. The insane racing of a heart which seemed about to burst from my chest, the sudden slick of sweat on my forehead, the shaking of my hands. Out of a clear blue sky for no apparent reason I felt terrified. A feeling of helplessness overwhelmed me, my face twisted up and I just wanted to cry. I had no idea what was happening to me.

I was surrounded by people and unable to move. My mind was racing as much as my heart. My body felt as if it had stalled and no power would be able to move it again. Then something happened which I've thought about a lot of times since. A guy minding the gate called over to me, 'Eamonn Sweeney, the *Cork Examiner*, do you want to take a shortcut across to the press box?'

I've never got an invitation like that before or since. And I've always wondered if this man saw what was happening to me and decided to help me out or if it was just a stroke of luck. I walked through the open gate and down the sideline, sneaking a Xanax into my mouth. Cork and Kerry were playing a junior championship match and I stopped behind the goals, taking in the fine spectacle of the Cork and Kerry colours competing on the kind of grass whose brilliant green colour is praised by every American who hits this neck of the woods. Entering the press box, I still felt shaky. Sweat coursed down my face and my back like I was a high-strung horse lathering up in the parade ring. I got my report written all the same.

After that it just felt like my batteries were running down. I felt constantly exhausted and on a couple of occasions in Skibbereen I went back to the car so I could lie down on the back seat. Fear of another attack kept me at home for the following two Sundays. Perhaps all I needed was rest. Or a change of scenery.

The big match on the Sunday after that was Sligo at home to Galway, which I fancied seeing as my native county had just beaten Mayo for the first time in a quarter century. I could stay with my mother and sister, who were both still living in Sligo at that stage, for a bit.

On the Friday evening, I was in the passenger seat of a car stopped at a set of traffic lights on the South Ring Road in Cork city when another fit of fright led me to leap out and sprint across the road like a fugitive fleeing a prison van.

I made my way to the city centre and booked into the Imperial Hotel where I spent the whole night awake, racked by tremendous chest pains and in a state of total terror. The pains continued the next morning, and it felt like I'd never leave the bed. I remember Venus Williams was playing Lindsay Davenport in the women's singles final at Wimbledon when a friend arrived to help me down the stairs and bundle me into a car. We set off for Sligo. I lay in the back and took occasional sups from a bottle of wine. I hadn't the energy for another escape.

The concerned look on my family's face when I shuffled into the house expressed everything they were too diplomatic to say out loud. Things went downhill after that. Sligo lost by eighteen points, and when I went for lunch in Murray's pub the following day, who was there only Brendan Gleeson. He'd come down to play some music, south Sligo being, as Matt Molloy said in the notes to one of his albums, 'rich in flute and fiddle music and nothing else'. The result is that I've never been able to enjoy watching him since. It's my loss.

A local doctor told me I might be better off back in the familiar surroundings of west Cork. He gave me Xanax and Tranxene, and I travelled back down south and collapsed. I was at the end of my rope.

My memories of the next couple of months revolve around a collapsible deck chair which I'd sit on in the garden if the day was fine (my memory is of a particularly good summer). I would stare at the sky in a stunned fashion for hours. Sometimes I'd think that it would be nice to get out of the chair and do something else but find myself entirely unable to move. I'd try to get up but I couldn't have got out of that chair if it had been on fire. That's how drained I was. Fifty yards up the street was the village shop operated by a friend of mine with whom I'd shared many enjoyable sporting chats. I couldn't get there – the small walk up the hill was too terrible to contemplate. So I stayed in my chair, unable to even read because my mind, which somehow managed to be both dulled and racing, couldn't concentrate on anything but its own disorder. When darkness fell, I exited the chair by tilting myself out of it and crawling on my hands and knees back into the house.

The nights were the worst. Utterly unable to sleep, I'd surrender after a couple of hours, hobble downstairs, lie on the couch and wait for the birds to announce the arrival of dawn. I couldn't focus sufficiently to watch a movie, though sometimes I'd put on a Euronews bulletin which seemed to run through the night and had a kind of eerie disembodied quality to it, like the sound didn't exactly fit with the pictures. The whole experience felt oddly like being underwater in a swimming pool as normal life carries on overhead behind the aqueous curtain.

An Eastern European dissident said that the worst bit about living under a dictatorship was not the everyday repression but the feeling that things would go on like this forever. Looking back at the dates, I see the whole episode lasted less than three months. I was back in the press box for the Galway–Kildare football semi-final at the end of August.

Had I been told it would only last that long maybe I'd have handled it better, gritted my teeth and seen out the time, paced myself in some way. But the sensation of powerlessness was so overwhelming – it felt like this might last forever and become my new reality. The anti-depressants I'd been prescribed, Lustral, initially gave me shivering fits as though the Artane Boys Band were practising marching routines on my grave. My teeth would chatter spectacularly like I was Scooby-Doo hearing a ghost in the next room. I spent a lot of time crying, not the healthy cathartic kind of cry which brings relief but the kind of bitterly frustrated fitful one which gives you a headache and leaves you sadder.

I suspected this was what people called a nervous breakdown and felt a terrible sensation of personal failure that it had happened to me. Was I an insane person? King Lear's lines 'O let me not be mad, not mad, sweet heaven. Keep me in temper, I would not be mad' kept coming to mind. In hindsight, this seems a bit overwrought but at the time I wasn't just in a state of panic, I was also in the dark. The stigma surrounding the discussion of mental illness made it feel like you were on your own so that a frightening experience also became a lonely one.

Just four years later *The Road to Croker* came out. I never mentioned those events in it. In his novel *The Corrections*, which I read during the *Road to Croker* summer, Jonathan Franzen has a character named Gary worry that 'If the idea he was depressed gained currency he would forfeit his right to his opinions. He would forfeit his moral certainties; every word he spoke would become a symptom of disease; he would never win an argument.' That's pretty much how things stood at the time. Mental illness was something only the most courageous people admitted to, and I wasn't one of them.

Now I can see that forfeiting your moral certainties isn't a bad thing and that winning arguments is over-rated. But as a journalist eking out a precarious freelance living, the last thing I needed was people thinking my opinions were the product of mental imbalance. As it turned out, when I did tell a couple of sports editors down the line how things were they were extremely supportive. You live and learn, but at the time I hadn't learned.

By the end of August 2000, I'd recovered sufficiently for a return to work. A few months later I went to Prague and had a great time. I told myself I was better now but I couldn't lose the feeling that there might be another breakdown with my name on it out there. I was no longer at ease. It felt as though I'd pulled a mental hamstring which might go again if put under too much strain.

So, I gradually pulled in the horns over the next few years. The TV work I'd enjoyed doing for RTÉ eventually came to an end because the trip to Dublin seemed too much of an ordeal. I turned down offers to do readings or appear in panel discussions. The thing I feared was fear itself and its possible manifestation in the public arena. I became reclusive. Bit by bit, what began as a nervousness about travel blossomed first into fear and then into a fully fledged phobia.

3

It's a Small World

FLYING BIT THE DUST AFTER A 2001 EPISODE WHEN
I had such a spectacular panic attack that I was allowed to
leave a plane getting ready for take-off at Venice Marco Polo
Airport. If it had been a couple of months later, after 9/11, they
might have shot me. I got back to Ireland by train and boat. The
memory of the incident remained so terrifying I hadn't flown,
or left the country, since.

The walls closed in slowly. Boats went off the menu in 2003
after another panic attack on the ferry from Baltimore to Cape
Clear where I barely managed to resist leaping into the sea like
an escaping mermaid. Rail travel lasted another six years until
19 November 2009 when sitting on the Galway train to Dublin
awaiting departure I suffered an attack of such disorientating

strength and suddenness that I scrambled on to the platform without taking my bags with me.

There were still buses until suddenly there weren't, panic seizing me as I boarded one from Cork to Galway with my daughters shortly after Covid had subsided. A few days later I asked my sister to turn back as she drove us from Spiddal to Galway. This was one more journey I couldn't handle. As I don't drive myself I was now comprehensively stuck.

Only then did I admit there might be a problem. Anxiety had severely constricted my life and rendered the most routine of activities utterly agonising. Yet I still thought of my travel difficulties as a kind of minor quirk. They'd been going on for two decades but eventually I'd get round to solving the problem by sheer willpower. One of these days it would all come right.

I rang my doctor in Skibbereen and he sent me on a prescription for Xanax, which enabled me to get home. It also helped me rally over the next year and return to public transport. It seemed like the problem might be solved.

But on 28 July 2023 I finally felt the full force of what anxiety had been storing up for me. It was the Friday before Galway Race Week. I'd been up to see my mother and decided to return to Cork by train, a somewhat roundabout route which involves going from Galway to Limerick, from Limerick up to Limerick Junction and from there to Cork. I thought the practice would do me good. I'd made the same journey a couple of months earlier and enjoyed it, the slow pace of the train offering a nice view of the south Galway and Clare countryside. Now things were about to fall apart.

On my way to the station in Galway, I felt slightly off my game. The day was warm. I was sweating and a bit agitated. I told myself I'd fight through these feelings and relax when the train got going.

The train was packed. This threw me for a loop. It had been almost empty last time I'd made the journey. I'd had a bit of space to gather myself. The presence of so many people made me feel under pressure. The Limerick–Galway train is much smaller than an inter-city train and has a slightly claustrophobic feeling at the best of times. This was not the best of times. I sat down on one seat, then switched to another and another like Goldilocks searching for the one that was just right. I couldn't settle. The heart was hammering, the hands were shaking, the feeling of being on the brink of an abyss rose inexorably. Five minutes were left before the train pulled out. I just needed to last till then – I'd done it before. I checked my pulse. It was rattling away between 160 and 170 beats per minute. Crazy. The panic built with every second.

Then it happened. The thing I'd always dreaded most, the spiral into the kind of mania which sets people raving in the streets to be sectioned and locked up. It's almost impossible to explain but I imagined a light going on somewhere inside my head. It was as though I'd completely gone out of the world. It had no reality anymore and neither did I. A familiar automated voice said that the doors were about to close. I knew that if they did and the train started, this time I really would start to shout and to pound the doors and windows and scream to be let out. There was no riding out this one. I lunged for the door and hit the button. Time seemed to telescope as I waited to see if it was too late for the doors to open. I had never wanted anything more fervently than that they would. A hiss, a parting, a dive and I was on the platform.

I was terrified but, more than that, I felt dissociated from the world. I stood on the platform for a bit, my T-shirt now wringing with sweat, wondering what to do next or if there was anything which could be done next. Panic had been joined by paralysis, with paranoia quickly turning up to make a threesome.

I walked around the streets of Galway for a while trying to get some kind of grip. Other pedestrians had the unreality of painted figures on a backdrop. It seemed impossible to connect this city, this city I loved, with what I was going through. I felt like the maddest Sweeney since the legendary king Suibhne Geilt, who'd been driven by trauma to live in a tree. If there'd been a tree handy I'd gladly have gone up it at that moment. I felt as though my body were a cell in which I was imprisoned alongside someone who wished me only evil. I was in the last ditch. Somewhere along the line, Sweeney had gone comprehensively astray.

After a while I settled sufficiently to brave a taxi out to Spiddal. Sloping in the back door, it seemed impossible that I'd ever know peace of mind again.

I rang the doctor in Skibbereen. This time his forwarding of the prescription for the Xanax I hoped would get me home was accompanied by a certain reluctance. He asked me to come in to see him when I got back. Something had to be done. I couldn't go on like this. As he said it, I realised, maybe for the first time, that he was right. Things *really* couldn't go on like this.

A week later the Xanax got me home. Just about. The journey was a nightmarish meander during which I baulked at getting the first bus and got off the second one in Limerick before phoning a friend to beg for a lift home from Cork, something I would never normally have done. I told her I didn't think I could make it any further. I was talking about the specific journey but it summed up my general state of mind as well.

I didn't know if I was nuts but I did know the way I'd been not dealing with the problem was. I had a good long chat with the doctor, who recommended medication and counselling by a clinical psychologist. Initially I resisted the first option even though it had helped me twenty-three years earlier. It seemed like an admission of defeat. I worried that it might alter my personality so that I was no longer the real me.

Then I realised that admitting defeat is no shame if you've actually been beaten. No point doing the Trump on it by inciting the rioters of denial to rampage through the Capitol of your consciousness. The idea that there's some irreducible core deep within containing the Real You seems dubious too. We're always remaking and remodelling ourselves. How real anyway was the person I'd been turned into by anxiety, afraid of travel and perpetually waiting for an imaginary hammer to fall?

The medication seemed to take the edge off even if the counselling didn't do much for me. Despite several attempts, it's never really helped.

I felt a bit better but the confidence had taken a knock. Never again, I vowed, would I put myself in a position to go through what I'd suffered in Galway. I had tried my best to beat this thing, given it what seemed an honest shot and it had defeated me. Anyway, who needed to travel? Weren't Skibbereen and west Cork enough to be going on with? Don't people flock to the area every summer and wish they lived here? I'd be perfectly happy pottering around here for the rest of my life. I had my family, my pets, my books, my music, my movie collection. It was time to resign myself for good to the restricted life. Like a footballer settling for a point instead of a goal, it was time to take the wise option.

Perhaps I'd eventually have persuaded myself that this was rational analysis rather than unconditional surrender.

So when, ten weeks after the Galway debacle, my former editor from Hachette emailed me out of the blue and asked if I fancied doing a sequel to *The Road to Croker*, my first instinct was to say no.

So I ignored the email. A second one followed a few days later. I ignored that one too. Surely she'd go away now. Then one morning the phone rang and there she was on the other end. I resolved never to answer a call from an unfamiliar number again and considered telling her I had another project on the go. Anything to make this well-meaning but annoyingly determined woman leave me in peace.

Yet in that moment I realised how much I *wanted* to say yes to this out-of-the-blue offer. I hadn't written a book in decades and had entirely lost confidence in my ability to do so. This seemed a golden opportunity to prove myself wrong. The only thing stopping me was fear of the travel involved. Yet I couldn't find the words to explain it. No one outside my family knew about it. I resolved the conflict by saying I was interested and then behaving in a passive-aggressive manner which I hoped would make the editor give up on the idea while also absolving me of the responsibility for having said no. That didn't work. The calls kept coming. I kept not answering them. 'Ghosting', I believe the young people call it. Finally, the editor outlasted me. It was decision time. I had to make a call one way or the other.

It was my daughters who persuaded me in the end. They insisted it was a fantastic opportunity. Writing the book would force me out of my comfort zone. Only then could

I confront my problems. If I didn't do it, they said, I'd regret it.

I've never been able to refuse them anything and so I said yes. With no idea how someone with a debilitating travel phobia could traverse Ireland the following summer to follow the 2024 championships, I agreed to set out on the journey. That didn't mean I'd finish it.

4

Just after High Noon, Ardrahan

MY EFFORTS TO BREAK THE PHOBIA THAT HAD taken over my life began in earnest the morning after saying yes to the determined editor. At that moment, the fear of not fulfilling a contract, having to return an advance, being exposed as a fraud – these things scared me even more than my fear of travel. I also knew that if I spurned this opportunity, I could never again pretend that things really weren't that bad. The lie I'd lived with for so long would be well and truly exposed. And then what?

I decided to face down the terror the Galway debacle the previous July had reawakened in me and begin the road to recovery by taking the bus from Skibb to Clonakilty. Filled with new hope, I marched down to the bus stop in Market Street.

And stayed there. When the moment came to get on, I simply couldn't do it. This perfectly harmless West Cork Connect bus was, to my mind, a trap where terrible things could happen to me. Nameless and ill-defined things which seemed nevertheless very real.

We weren't off to a great start. But by December things were starting to change. The medication seemed to be working and, though they were still something of an ordeal, I was starting to take bus journeys again. Car journeys were fine too but the train remained the big stumbling block. Over Christmas in Spiddal I set a target of taking a train ride before returning to Cork in the New Year. If I hadn't made some kind of train journey by then it was time to consider throwing in the towel.

Twice I went to Galway station, bought a ticket as far as Athenry, walked on to the platform and turned back just before I reached the ticket collector. One more failure and that'd be that. I bought a third ticket to Athenry, turned back again and walked out of the station, feeling like a footballer with a terrible disciplinary record who's just got another red card.

Then, as I passed the Imperial Hotel and Supermac's, something made me turn back and retrace my steps. Someone, actually. Ivan Alexandrevich Goncharov, born Simbirsk 1821, died St Petersburg 1891.

Goncharov wrote one famous novel, *Oblomov*, which I happened to be reading that Christmas. The title character's dominant characteristic is an inability to ever get round to doing anything. He spends the start of the book trying to get out of bed and keeps failing. Some readers see him as a heroic slacker figure but to me there was something tragic about the story.

Oblomov is a lovable figure but his chronic reluctance to face the world sees him lose a wonderful woman he loves and who loves him, get swindled out of his money by conmen and end up losing his health as well. He knows he shouldn't be like this but he can't help it. It's not a deliberate decision, life just gets away from him. It's such a great novel that, as often happens, Oblomov assumed a certain reality for me. I'd have done anything to save him from his fate. Now it struck me that Oblomov's fate might be a precursor of my own. I couldn't change his but it wasn't too late to change mine.

I had an idea. To break the cycle, I could get a *bus* out of Galway to a destination with a train station. And from that new, unfamiliar place, I would board a train back to Galway. Anything was worth a shot.

Which is how, on 8 January 2024, I ended up waiting on a lonely platform in the remote Galway village of Ardrahan, as the train approached as though it were carrying a letter which might decide the rest of my life. It pulled in and I got on. This time I didn't dive for the doors. It was a promising start. As the train pulled away and headed towards Craughwell I braced myself. Now there was no escape. I was locked in the carriage with my fear. I waited for it to take over. At any moment, I could be plunged into panic. And not just any panic. The prospect of it had haunted me for years. It was an unchecked state that might see me beating against the doors screaming to be let out. I could make an utter public spectacle of myself, become the next viral TikTok sensation: 'Mad Irish Train Man'. The stress might lead to a full-blown heart attack. Any and all of this could happen. But it didn't.

Instead, to my amazement, the old familiar anxiety abated. I was possessed by a sudden calm. Instead of enduring the moment, I began to enjoy it. I looked out the window and there was something magnificent about this undistinguished stretch of countryside in south Galway. Its fields and ditches, its trees and cattle filled me with a sense of wonder. It was like I'd left my fears on the platform in Ardrahan. This was one of the best moments of my life.

Perhaps I'd manage this book after all.

5

A Stroll in the Páirc

IT WAS THE FIRST SUNDAY IN APRIL. STORM
Kathleen had lashed into us the night before but had rapidly
died away. I walked down to Páirc Uí Chaoimh to watch Cork
play Limerick in the Munster football championship. There
was a couple in their forties just ahead of me. The man carried
a hurl and pucked a sliotar ahead of him for a Jack Russell
terrier to chase. A sign informed us that the Marina Park would
eventually be five times the size of Fitzgerald Park. It seemed
typically Cork to point out how impressive something is by
comparing it with something else in the county.

In 2003 the stadium ahead of us, a concrete bowl apparently
inspired by the architecture of the Ceauşescu regime in
Romania, was renowned for its ugliness. But no more. Coming

into view was a handsome streamlined modern structure. Facelifts never come cheap but no one expected PUC II to be quite so expensive. Originally projected to cost sixty million euros, the redevelopment came in at over 100 million, placing Cork County Board in a perilous financial state.

So desperate was the board's need for money they'd proposed renaming the stadium SuperValu Park earlier in the year before a chorus of disapproval from supporters led to the compromise of SuperValu Páirc Uí Chaoimh. The strength of feeling against the change showed the difference between the GAA and the other big hitters of Irish sport. No one in rugby or soccer batted an eyelid when Lansdowne Road became the Aviva Stadium. But the general feeling among Cork GAA fans was that something important would be lost if the original proposal wasn't opposed. Replacing the name of Pádraig Ó Caoimh, a former War of Independence hero whose thirty-five years as GAA general secretary made him instrumental in the association becoming the great powerhouse of Irish sport, with that of a supermarket chain was seen as symbolically significant. One of the GAA's great strengths is its ability to adapt to the changing nature of Irish society. It is not an old-fashioned organisation. But it is one with a profound respect for tradition. This Janus-like ability to look simultaneously at past and future perhaps mirrors the country as a whole.

It wasn't just the stadium which had become more attractive in the last twenty years. The walk out to the pitch through a kind of industrial wasteland also used to be a grim affair. But this Sunday a host of people were sitting on deck chairs in front of the Marina Market, a former fruit company warehouse repurposed during the Covid pandemic. The market only survived an initial refusal of planning permission after a campaign which included a petition signed by 20,000 people. Watching families, with typical Irish optimism, taking what little sun there was while others bore away fancy burgers, ice cream and barbecued goods, it seemed like the right decision was made in the end. A temporary Funderland, with youngsters queuing up for contraptions which gave me vertigo just looking at them, added to the carnival atmosphere.

There wasn't an iota of suspense attached to the first game on the journey. Everyone knew Limerick hadn't a hope. They'd lost all seven matches en route to relegation from division three. Only six of the nineteen players who appeared in their last Munster championship game were still on the team. It was a far cry from 2003 when Limerick, in their brief football county moment, trounced Cork by eight points.

Cork were managed by John Cleary who popped up in the final pages of the original book, offering me a lift to Union Hall for the celebrations of Castlehaven's 2003 county senior championship victory. Off I went for a night which brought home to me just how much such victories meant to local communities.

John's father Ned was a garda from Ballindine in Mayo. Sent to Castletownshend in 1962, he first joined the Castlehaven club and then set about transforming it. In 1969 he managed the team to a divisional Junior B title, not the most prestigious title but the beginning of a journey which would bring the little club to a first county senior final in 1979 and a first county senior title in 1989, the repetition of those nines lending this progress the air of a masterplan. Cork had never seen anything like it. The exclamation of a city opponent, 'we didn't come down here to get beaten by a bunch of farmers', showed the jolt this long march represented to the status quo.

It takes a community to build a club yet Ned Cleary was the prime mover behind it all, a figure so central it was possible to imagine an alternative history where he'd been transferred somewhere else and that village reaped the benefit.

The man built not just a club but a clan. In 2023 he and his wife Kathleen's grandchildren played for Cork in the senior football championship (Rory Maguire), the senior hurling championship (Damien and Conor Cahalane), the senior camogie championship (Méabh and Orlaith Cahalane) and the senior ladies' football championship (Emma Cleary and Orlaith Cahalane). His son John won two All-Ireland senior football medals while his daughter Nollaig racked up nine from 2005 to 2014 with the all-conquering Cork ladies' team.

Ned and Kathleen seemed to be forever following the fortunes of their grandchildren up and down the country. It seemed like a fantastic life. They exuded such irrepressible enthusiasm and vitality that my first thought on hearing of Ned's death in March 2021 was that it had come much too soon. He was ninety. Kathleen is still supporting the family.

Now John was managing Cork, though, like King Charles, there was a sense of him coming very late to the throne. In 2009 he'd managed the Cork under-21 team to an All-Ireland title. In the semi-final they'd beaten a Dublin side managed by Jim Gavin. Gavin steered Dublin to an All-Ireland the following year and was appointed senior manager in 2012.

So when the Cork job became vacant in 2013, Cleary, who'd added three Munster titles to that All-Ireland, was the obvious candidate. He didn't get it. As Cork embarked on a precipitous decline, new managers were appointed again in 2015 and 2017.

He remained the obvious candidate but Cork County Board appeared to have adopted an ABC (Anyone But Cleary) policy. His face just didn't fit.

When in 2021 Cork appointed Keith Ricken, the first manager to win an All-Ireland under-21, now under-20, title since Cleary, the perpetual contender's time seemed to have passed for good. It was a nice surprise when Ricken appointed Cleary as a coach. He might never get the manager's job but at least he'd be involved.

Then, just before the 2022 championship, Ricken resigned. Cleary stepped in as interim boss and stayed on as manager. Almost a decade late, the reins were finally in his hands. I was pleased for him, as I was pleased to see another Castlehaven man, Brian Hurley, captain the side.

In 2012, Brian had kicked twelve points, five from play, against Nemo in the county final. He was twenty, a prodigy apparently destined to become a household name. It hadn't quite worked out like that. His career had been decent with some notable highlights but also included two horrendous hamstring injuries which almost forced him into retirement aged twenty-five.

Looking at him play, I feel the kind of proprietary worry which afflicts everyone watching a player from their club on the inter-county stage. I feel the same thing when watching Damien Cahalane, who I also knew as a teenager, play for the Cork hurlers. There's a feeling of almost personal implication, pride when they do well but an even greater fear that they won't. You contest every ball with them in a way you don't with anyone else. Journalists have a version of this where they dread the possibility of a player they've interviewed during the week going badly. Because the manager may well blame the interview, the player will feel bad and the journalist, though he knows this is daft, will deep down feel kind of responsible.

Brian led out Cork and the cheery Europop of 'Freed from Desire' and 'I Gotta Feeling' struck an incongruous note as the rain briefly spat and a strong wind got up. Then the national anthem issued from the PA system and as we faced the flag, though I would claim to be the least nationalist of people, I felt unmistakably joined in a bond of mutual sympathy with everyone here. Whatever it was, whatever this moment meant, I was part of it and could not deny it even if I wanted to.

The big question was not whether Cork would win but whether the match would be over at half-time. The omens weren't good when home wing-back Mattie Taylor strode up to score the first point of my 2024 championship after just twenty seconds. Cork, stronger, quicker and just better, could have put the game to bed in the first ten minutes but, after moving the ball impressively through the defence, botched three clear goal chances.

Limerick took courage from their reprieve, aided by a 'you'd want a lead with that behind you' breeze which helped them bang over a few fine points from long range. After surviving another couple of close shaves, they led by one at the break. Nobody thought this portended a shock but it seemed a small triumph of resistance.

After half-time Cork quickly moved two points clear and Limerick found themselves caught in a bind. One of the main topics of conversation after the previous year's championship had been the move towards a style where teams used short passes to hold possession for long spells, often travelling laterally or backwards and at half-pace in an effort to engineer an opening against a blanket defence. The result was often stasis and utter boredom for the spectators. Former Armagh player Aaron Kernan described how fans often chatted among themselves or checked their phones while these labyrinthine moves unfolded.

Even the tactics nerds who'd exhorted sceptics to admire the new style because it was how football had 'evolved' were embarrassed by now. The establishment of a Football Review Committee, chaired by Jim Gavin, was a response to the diminishing attractiveness of the game. It was expected to report at the end of the season with recommendations for rule changes.

For the moment we were stuck with something which often degenerated into a kind of gridlock, especially when a team didn't have the ability to get anywhere against the opposition defence. For two and a half minutes Limerick passed the ball over and across, backwards and forwards without getting anywhere.

It was an accident waiting to happen. Eventually they lost the ball, Cork counter-attacked and Chris Óg Jones scored a goal to effectively end the game as a contest. The Rebels were five points up with almost half an hour left and the anticipated massacre seemed about to transpire.

It didn't because Limerick hung doggedly in there for a long time. It was remarkable when you thought about it. Here was a team with no hope of winning anything yet its members had obviously done the work to achieve an astounding level of fitness for amateur players.

The modern possession-based game requires that fitness, yet even though Cork were much better than their opposition, they weren't running away from them and Limerick weren't wilting.

You can see why someone pushes themselves hard in a county where there's a chance of glory and recognition. But what was in it for the Limerick footballer? Why did he breach the pain barrier in training night after night? A combination of personal and local pride coupled with loyalty to his team-mates perhaps. There's a stubborn selflessness there which seems wholly admirable. It's the only way the show stays on the road in the counties doomed to almost eternal underdog status. I found myself rooting for Limerick. Not to win, because that was obviously impossible, but to keep the score down. They were still just four points behind with eight minutes left before two Cork goals in quick succession pushed the winning margin out to eleven points, 3–13 to 0–11.

There'd be bigger challenges ahead for the winners, yet I felt like Limerick had taken what small glory was available in this game. By leading at half-time and not crumbling after they'd fallen behind in the second half they'd kept some pride. I come from Sligo whose history also consisted largely of enduring through thin and thin. So I knew that while not losing by as much as expected could never be a victory, it wasn't a worthless result either. Youngsters are often advised to learn life lessons from the example of sporting champions. But the lessons available from the also-rans can be pretty valuable too. Like Limerick, we all have days when the best we can do is make an impossible situation a bit more bearable.

It was good to be back on the road.

6

The Rural Kid

PORTLAOISE GETS A BAD RAP. SO DOES THE midlands in general. En route to the Leinster football championship game between Laois and Offaly I got an email from one of my daughters: *Enjoy all that the midlands has to offer. That should take you about five minutes.*

The midlands is Ireland's red-headed stepchild. Portlaoise is the midlands of the midlands.

In the early noughties I had a mild disagreement on RTÉ's *Questions and Answers* with a conservationist who regarded one-off rural housing as a very great evil. Months later I met him on the Dublin–Cork bus. He was still very cross, and as I was getting off the bus at Portlaoise, he pointed out the window at an unremarkable collection of shops and shouted at me, 'Look at it, look at it. That's James Fintan Lalor Avenue Portlaoise, the worst piece of development in Ireland. This is the kind of thing you want.'

I suspected that he regarded my decision to voluntarily visit Portlaoise, for a Wexford–Tyrone national football league semi-final, as confirmation of my irredeemable redneck status. But I'm in good, or at least famous, company. Back in 2014 Kanye West and Kim Kardashian's first stop on their Irish honeymoon was the town's Odeon Cinema, where they took in *X-Men: Days of Future Past*. How differently it might have turned out for them had they opted to stay in Portlaoise rather than return to LA.

The championship wasn't the only big contest of the summer. Local and European elections loomed with the latter contested by a slate of candidates whose eclectic nature reflected the political turmoil in the air. One of them was canvassing outside O'Moore Park. I made my way over to him on the grounds of personal acquaintance rather than political sympathy, because myself and Ciaran Mullooly, the Independent Ireland candidate, went back a long way. We're not friends or enemies but we worked in Longford at the same time, he with Shannonside Radio, me with the *Longford News*, and found ourselves at a lot of the same matches and meetings.

As RTÉ's regional correspondent Mullooly was kind of Mr Midlands in the same way that Jim Fahy in the west, Eileen Magnier in the north-west and Paschal Sheehy in the south-west were seen not just as reporters, but as ambassadors. Spend long enough trying to persuade those running a broadcaster with a heavy metropolitan bias that stories from your bailiwick are important and you inevitably become an advocate for its virtues.

Normally a very self-assured man (that big voice isn't put on for TV – he talks like that all the time), Mullooly seemed nervous. Addressing people from your platform on national television is very different to asking for their vote outside a GAA ground. It's easy to mistake celebrity for popularity but elections tell you what people really think of you. Rejection at the ballot box is as personally brutal as in a love affair.

He said someone told him it was time to get off the fence. Since leaving RTÉ a few years before, he'd been working in local development and tourism initiatives. The closure of the ESB power station in his native Lanesboro hit him hard. 'My brother worked there,' he told me.

Ciaran's brother Pat died of a heart attack in his forties. I remember him for two reasons. One was the goal he scored in Carrick-on-Shannon in the 1982 division four play-off to give Longford a win over Sligo. It was one of those fantastic goals where a full-forward gets to the ball just ahead of the full-back, shoots instantly on the turn and sticks it in the top corner.

Just over a decade later I had a couple of pints with Ciaran and Pat in Andy Byrne's pub in Longford town. There was a debate about some football statistic. It turned out Pat was right and I was wrong. 'You can't beat the rural kid,' he exclaimed gleefully. I loved that saying so much it's become a kind of family catchphrase.

Perhaps it also captured the spirit of Independent Ireland and the other rural independents whose support was running at an all-time high in the run-up to the local and European elections. Some people believed Independent Ireland might become an Irish version of Germany's AfD or other European far-right parties. Their recruitment of Niall Boylan, a Dublin radio shock jock with a bee in his bonnet about immigration and transgender rights, was hardly reassuring.

Yet Mullooly's spiel about rural Ireland's development being stifled by too little funding and too much EU bureaucracy was one he'd been delivering for a long time. He'd written a book on the subject long before entering politics. Thirty years previously we'd both covered a march to the Dáil protesting against plans to terminate the Sligo–Dublin railway line at Mullingar. The idea seems insane now but it was a runner at the time and the marchers believed they were, in the words of one organiser, being treated like 'gumpkins'. Support for Collins and Mullooly, as opposed to Boylan, seemed like the familiar Irish phenomenon of rural resentment at perceived urban condescension. The rural kid didn't want to get beaten anymore. Independent Ireland's politics weren't mine but I wished Mullooly well and meant it because I knew him. We're Irish. That's how we roll.

Laois were favourites and Offaly hadn't beaten them in

O'Moore Park since 1978 but they were already four points up when Laois defender James Kelly, in the words of the *Offaly Express*, 'let the elbow back' and got the red card for it. The home team seemed suddenly spurred on by the loss of a man and were level by the break.

But all hope went out the window six minutes into the second half when Laois made such a mess of a short kick-out that Offaly's Keith O'Neill ended up facing an empty net and rolled the ball into it.

The second Offaly goal four minutes later was much more spectacular. Laois had pushed so many players forward that when they lost the ball a quick Offaly pass found wing-forward Jordan Hayes on the half-way line with nothing in front of him but an expanse of grass and the Laois goal in the distance.

A chase commenced which resembled Wile E. Coyote's pursuit of the Road Runner. Two defenders gained on Hayes, who had to solo the ball as well as run, and appeared almost close enough to bring him crashing to the ground. You could nearly see their breath ruffling the back of his jersey, yet he kept that half-step ahead and his shot past Laois keeper Killian Roche brought the biggest cheer of the night.

Offaly ran out 2–13 to 1–8 winners. That was as good as it got for them. Ahead lay a hammering by Dublin and a humiliating home defeat by London.

Still, like Kanye and Kim, they'd always have Portlaoise. Who could ask for anything more?

7

David Clifford, Superstar

FITZGERALD STADIUM KILLARNEY IS THE MOST beautiful Irish sporting venue. Thurles has more history and Croke Park is more important but Fitzgerald Stadium trumps both for aesthetic appeal. Standing on the terraces on a fine day with the mountains in the distance giving the ground an amphitheatre air, you can see why people have come from all over for more than a hundred years to look at these views.

On our way to the Munster final between Cork and Kerry we luxuriated in the year's first real blast of sunshine, basking as only Irish people can in the balmy furnace heat of eighteen degrees centigrade. The streets were full of people in the typical GAA summer pose of carrying a coat on their arm because you never know when the weather might change. I was one of them.

From the Cork to Kerry bus we watched the men of the Lee Valley perpetrating the first cut of the summer, laboriously propelling out-of-practice lawnmowers through recalcitrant grass which had bulked up in the gym of spring. As we passed one garden so overgrown you could have filmed a Vietnam War movie in it, one of the lads in the seat behind me quipped, 'He mustn't have got the memo.'

The lads, rangy athletic-looking dudes you'd have picked out as Gaelic footballers if you'd run into them crossing the Sahara Desert, were in high spirits. Unwrapping sandwiches and cracking open cans of beer before we even left the city, their conversation was almost entirely about football. Not the game so much as the ancillary stuff which might make you better at it. The effectiveness of various physiotherapists was discussed, the relative benefits of yoga and Pilates compared, the benefits of sports psychology pondered. It was an eye-opener for someone from an era when match preparation consisted of turning up for your lift and not forgetting your boots.

The bus disgorged us into Killarney, which as always seemed to have been prepared by a director eager to film the best possible traditional big-match atmosphere. A guy with a mobile grill was selling burgers out the back of his car, another man was playing the banjo, and a crowd of drinkers were spilling out to the road from the footpath outside the McSweeney Arms Hotel. The customary throng outside McSweeney's is always the first image that springs to mind when I think of Killarney.

Good-humoured, boisterous and humming with expectation, the crowd encapsulates the town's matchday spirit. This was Fleadh Peil na Mumhan.

Like a man who'd been tied to one of the town's lamp-posts during his stag do, I was returning to Killarney with mixed emotions. Would the old feelings lie in wait like snipers? I steeled myself for the tremulousness to begin. It didn't. Walking into the ground I thought, *I'm in*, like a hacker cracking the password which gives him access to the bad guys' computer system.

The descriptions of the grand old rivalry between Cork and Kerry which preceded their championship meetings had developed a somewhat dutiful tone. In reality Kerry–Cork has a colonial domination feel to it, the powerful empire putting down sporadic uprisings by a subject people with considerable cruelty.

Going into that Saturday's game, Kerry had won ten of the previous eleven meetings. The circumstances surrounding Cork's win in 2020, a last-second goal, an empty stadium thanks to Covid, an apocalyptic thunderstorm, were so freakish they seemed to underline how extraordinary the result was these days. Kerry won by twenty-two points in 2021, by seventeen in 2018, by twelve in 2022. Reducing the margin to two the previous year in Páirc Uí Chaoimh represented a considerable achievement on Cleary's part but Killarney was a horse pulling a jaunting cart of a different colour. Every Cork fan was aware of the potential for humiliation.

Instead Cork went into 'cry havoc and let slip the dogs of war' mode from the off, running at the heart of the defence, moving the ball quickly and ripping right through Kerry. They should have scored a goal in the first minute but Conor Corbett put his shot over. Five minutes later Ian Maguire rampaged down the middle and this time Paul Walsh slotted the ball home. Who'd seen this coming?

By the end of the first quarter Cork were still four points up, with their supporters greatly cheered by the misfortunes of David Clifford. These were misfortunes in a relative sense. Nothing demonstrates Clifford's status like the way opposition fans cheer a misplaced pass or a wide on his part as though it were a score for their own team. That Cork had dispossessed him three times in that first quarter seemed a victory in itself.

I'd never seen that happen with any other player. But everything about Clifford had always been different. He was the first player whose arrival in senior ranks had been accompanied by the type of great expectations more familiar from the drafting of a college phenomenon into the NFL or NBA. While still playing minor he'd been attracting the GAA equivalent of the famous 'I saw rock and roll future and its name is Bruce Springsteen' line from *Rolling Stone*.

In his final minor year, when he scored six points from play in both the Munster final and All-Ireland quarter-final, 1–7 from play in the semi and an astounding 4–4 in the final, he looked like a senior star surreptitiously smuggled into the competition. His senior debut, in an otherwise unremarkable 2018 national league opener against Donegal, was treated as a major occasion.

The unprecedented level of hype meant Clifford faced an almost impossible task in living up to expectations. Yet he succeeded. An All-Star in his first senior year, he was Player of the Year and an All-Ireland winner in his fourth. By the age of twenty-three his claim to be considered the greatest footballer of all time could be debated but not dismissed. There was something larger than life about the kid. A legendary aura similar to the one which had once surrounded Christy Ring and Mick O'Connell already hovered over him.

Clifford seemed the ultimate expression of his game's capacity for beauty. You could say that a computer asked to design the perfect Gaelic footballer might come up with David Clifford. But that was too mechanical a description of a player with such a flair for inspired improvisation. One moment in the 2023 qualifier meeting with Tyrone encapsulated this element in his armoury.

Sprinting towards a ball played down the left sideline fifty yards from goal with two defenders converging upon him, Clifford seemed sure to be either bottled up or shouldered into touch once he took possession. But instead of catching the ball he flicked it down onto his left foot and hooked a thirty-yard pass down the wing to Tony Brosnan while still heading towards the line. The move ended with a goal for

Seán O'Shea and cemented the idea of Clifford as the genius who successfully executed moves his peers wouldn't even have thought of.

Yet just three weeks separated this tour de force from the game which, for the first time, suggested a chink in the Clifford armour. Frustrated for much of the All-Ireland final against Dublin by a poor supply of ball and a sterling man-marking performance by canny veteran Michael Fitzsimons, he might still have won it for Kerry.

Yet in the final quarter with the game up for grabs he missed a number of good chances, was visibly forcing things and couldn't exert his will on the game in the usual manner as Dublin edged it by two points. It wasn't a terrible performance but genius creates the standards by which it will be judged and from this point of view Clifford had come up short.

For the first time he would begin a season with a point to prove. Clifford's reputation had not been diminished by the defeat – he won a second successive Player of the Year award – but it felt as if the final represented a certain loss of innocence for player and supporters alike.

It wasn't just Clifford's talent but the attention paid to that talent which was unprecedented. A photo of him enveloped by young autograph-seekers following a routine league game in Roscommon was a reminder that no GAA star has ever had to go through anything like this before. Wherever he played, the youngsters waited like greyhounds in the traps for the final whistle, sprinted towards him and were greeted with great courtesy and patience.

Clifford came from the small village of Fossa, four miles outside Killarney, whose other famous native was the actor Michael Fassbender. It sometimes seemed that Clifford's level of fame had more in common, in Ireland at least, with Fassbender's than with that of any other footballer. The difference was that Fassbender's fame was part of the deal actors struck with Hollywood. His fellow Fossonian could hardly have imagined playing football would lead to this. He wasn't a movie star or even a professional sportsman. Celebrity was part of Fassbender's full-time job but Clifford had to balance it with work as a PE teacher in St Brendan's College, Killarney.

His Fossa roots made Clifford's story even better. The generational talent had come from one of those tiny clubs for whom survival rather than silverware is usually the measure of success. His materialisation on the shores of Lough Leane was a bit like Clark Kent's sudden arrival in the town of Smallville, Kansas.

In 2022 he'd contributed huge scores as the club won their first ever Kerry premier junior championship. They went on to win the All-Ireland title but it meant Clifford, who'd also helped East Kerry win the county senior crown, ended up playing football for almost a year without a break.

It had been a gruelling year off the field too. A photo taken after the 2022 All-Ireland final showed David and his mother

Ellen reaching to embrace each other after Kerry's victory. It encapsulated the joy of a parent in seeing a child succeed, the gratitude of the child for that joy and the shared history which lends so much extra weight to the moment. It was a beautiful thing.

Less than a year later Ellen Clifford passed away from cancer at the age of sixty. 'It could never be about her, it had always to be about us,' David remembered. 'Even at her sickest she'd always still be talking about how we were fixed for the weekend. She was so selfless like that.' He'd become a parent himself, Óigí, his son with partner Shauna O'Connor, turning two a month after Ellen's death. That, as any father or mother will tell you, has its challenges as well as its joys, especially in the early sleepless days. And nights. So many nights.

The huge expectations, the unparalleled attention, the back-breaking schedule, the family tragedy, the pressures of a first job and a first child. Watching Clifford lose the ball three times in that first quarter I wondered if it might all become too much even for him.

So when, three minutes before the break, he found himself in space forty yards out and landed a beautiful point, I felt strangely relieved.

Five minutes earlier Cork had been four points up. Though they still led by a point at half-time, they probably lost the game in the final ten minutes of the first half. Having troubled Kerry with the abandon and exuberance of their running game, Cork began to slow things down. You saw the team which began the game in 'we've nothing to lose, let's give this a real rattle' mode start to think 'let's not do anything hasty here, we've got something to hold on to'. It was the eternal underdog dilemma. How can you keep playing like you've nothing to lose when playing like you've nothing to lose has put you in a place where you have something to lose?

Cork didn't do anything terribly wrong in the second half but it gradually became impossible to imagine them as winners. Twenty minutes from time Kerry took the lead with another nice Clifford point, his third from play. The margin between the teams varied between one and three points but there was an abiding sense of Kerry being in control. Their bouts of possession football made my attention waver and I took note of my terrace companions. There was a boy, nine or ten years old, who spoke entirely in sports cliches: 'Come on, Kerry, don't allow them to regain their composure.' Fellow feeling brought back memories of perching in front of the telly at the same age writing a real-time report of the 1978 All-Ireland football final between Kerry and Dublin in a copybook with a round tower on the front. I probably mentioned composure too. That's the kind of kid I was.

Kerry won by three in the end. Cork had regained some pride after losing by twenty-two points on their previous visit to Killarney. I was pleased for John Cleary and also for Brian Hurley who kicked four from play and was the Rebels' best player. It was now going on thirty years since Cork had won in Fitzgerald Stadium. Back at the bus station I discovered I'd lost my ticket. When I tried to buy another one the driver told me the bus, the last one of the day, was booked out. I wandered across to the railway station where a special matchday train was waiting on the platform. This should have been a stroke of luck but it wasn't quite as simple as that.

My return to rail travel had been aided by magical thinking on my part. I would wait till a couple of minutes before the scheduled departure time, when the final call would send me dashing for the train. That way I didn't have much time to think about getting off again. By the time I'd found a seat and settled myself down, the tell-tale jerk would set the train going and it'd be too late to back out. It may sound absurd but the ritual was working for me and I had no plans to change it.

Now I was faced with a train which would not move till sufficient numbers of homebound fans had boarded. I wouldn't be waiting two minutes – I'd have to wait in my seat for five or ten or maybe half an hour with the possibility of the tension mounting and prompting an ignominious exit. I dallied on the platform, pondering the possibilities of an overnight stay in Killarney or even a taxi over the mountains as far as Bantry. After all, these were special circumstances and this was not an ordinary scheduled train, so backing away from it would not really constitute a defeat. Would it?

I knew the answer to the question and knew there was no

guarantee this summer journey would always let me remain in my comfort zone. I'm aware how ludicrous it was to be steeling myself for a train trip between Cork and Killarney like Michael Palin weighing up the pros and cons of taking a dhow across the Arabian Sea. But this was where I was at. I bought my ticket and walked on to the platform.

'We're sending them home very quiet,' a railwayman observed gleefully as the Cork fans filed towards the train. There was an undeniable beaten-army-in-retreat feeling.

The train was quiet except for a gang of young women in Cork jerseys singing 'Man! I Feel Like a Woman' by Shania Twain, again and again. And again.

They detoured into 'Pretty Woman' but, unable to remember much of that beyond the bit where the titular character walks down the street, quickly returned to Shania's timeless anthem of female solidarity.

It was, as us old-timers like to say, nice to see the young people enjoying themselves. As they sang and I waited five, ten, fifteen minutes for the train to depart, my anticipated tremulousness failed to arrive. For the first time in decades I was able to sit on a stationary train without feeling any discomfort. It was another step forward.

For the remainder of the season, not a day went by without my thinking of that song. Walking to the ground, standing on the terraces, perusing the programme, during lulls in the action, it would materialise unbidden in my mind's ear. This wasn't just a matchday thing. Walking the dog, washing the dishes, cooking the dinner, hoovering the carpet, reading a book, writing this book, I'm ambushed by it. I'm suffering from PTSD, Persistent Twain Song Disorder. But in a good way.

Because as 'Man! I Feel Like a Woman' carried us out of Killarney, across the border and all the way back to Kent Station I realised that, while I mightn't be the mentally strongest person on the train, I wasn't crazy. Not todally.

8

Muintir an Tuar

HALF A MILE OUT THE MAIN ROAD WEST OF SPIDDAL is a right turn that's easy to miss. Drivers given insufficient warning shoot past it and must retrace their tracks. The turn leads on to a boreen with the traditional features: narrowness, a bumpy surface and a strip of grass down the middle.

There are just half a dozen houses in Tuar Beag but sometimes I've thought of it as encapsulating the spirit of not just the GAA but Ireland in general. I remember walking up one summer Sunday and hearing the RTÉ match commentary from Eddie Sheáinín's house at the bottom of the boreen. A hundred yards further on a different description issued from the house of Taimín Dan, one of those traditionalists who'd turn down the TV and opt for the words of Mícheál Ó Muircheartaigh on radio. Further on up the hill they were listening to the match in Mikeen Dan's and across the road I could hear Marty Morrissey shouting the odds from the last house in Tuar Beag. Its sole inhabitant was born on this boreen, lives there and will probably die there too. Evelyn Sweeney, daughter of Máirtín and Peige Feeney, Máirtín Ned Mháire and Peige Bheartla Séamus Thaidhg as they were known. My mother.

Other days I'd walk up that boreen and stop to talk to Eddie, almost always about sport and generally about the GAA. I might chat to Mikeen Dan, who'd once played for Dublin Corporation in an inter-firms game at Croke Park, the fact that my mother kept shouting 'Come on, Tex' distracting him as he wondered which spectator knew his Spiddal nickname. Mikeen, who'd once been the local postman, died last year at the age of ninety-one and Tuar Beag seems diminished without him, though he remains a presence. His wife, Máire Pheter, is a talented actor who appeared for many years in TG4's *Ros na Rún* and Raidió na Gaeltachta's *Baile an Droichead*.

I've walked this boreen since I was a small child. Back then Eddie Sheáinín's mother, known as Baibín, had a small sweet shop where his house stands now. It was a cool dark haven abounding in plastic jars filled with boiled sweets and lent a magical air by my reading of Hansel and Gretel. I would imagine spells being cast there in the same way that I used to push through the hanging coats in various family wardrobes in the hope of finding Narnia behind them.

The next two houses, Dan's and Tom's, were distinguished in my mind by their two contrasting patriarchs. Tom survived longest of the three men who seemed to dominate the boreen. I remember going down to Tom's house on the night of my grandfather's funeral to fetch extra chairs for the crowd and being left in his wake as he bounded up the road draped with furniture.

Dan was a more distant figure who in my memory stands in the door of his house looking out towards the sea through his glasses as though pondering important questions. The story that Michael Collins had stayed there, Dan's brother Mícheál having been a senior figure in the Connemara Brigade of the Old IRA, gave this simple stone house a certain mystique. Stories about the War of Independence, how the Black and Tans spat at my grandmother and her friends as they walked to school, how my grandfather and his friends had hidden in a ditch one night when the Tans went on the rampage, how a local man who'd been captured was stripped naked and dragged across a large rock on a local beach, were omnipresent.

Long memories turned history into current affairs. Aged seven I was shocked when my grandmother expressed pleasure at the death of Éamon de Valera – an event marked by an almost complete Soviet-style shutdown of the nation's one television channel – on the grounds that he'd been ultimately responsible for the death of Michael Collins. The tumultuous nation-founding days of the twenties, an almost prehistoric era to a child, were as far away then as the seventies are now. There's a lot I remember from the seventies.

A couple of years back Eddie Sheáinín erected a sign at the bottom of the boreen wishing the local GAA club, Mícheál Breathnach's, best of luck 'Ó Muintir an Tuar'. I probably don't qualify as a member of that fraternity but I feel more at home in Spiddal than anywhere else. In my native south Sligo village of Gurteen I always had the feeling, as the son of parents from Galway and Kilkenny, of being a 'blow-in'. There were no other relations nearby whereas in Spiddal, where we spent most summer holidays, I had uncles, aunts and cousins.

It was in Spiddal that my Uncle Ned may have set my seven-year-old self on his future career path by giving me a *Guinness Book of Sports Records* which became a constant companion for years until basically falling apart from use. It was an American book and I pored over stats about baseball, American football, basketball and ice hockey long before I saw any of these games being played. That interest in stateside sport has never left me and one of the great pleasures of my life has been the NFL Sundays when myself and my daughter Lara watch the nine o'clock game on Sky accompanied by hot dogs and various items of American confectionery sold at an exorbitant price in the local SuperValu.

In my mind Ned forever executes his favourite move, a stepover followed by a shot with the side of his foot, outside my grandparents' house as we kick some plastic ball bought from Francis' shop in Spiddal where it had sat outside in the sun alongside flimsy nets on the end of thin sticks, buckets for making sandcastles and the plastic spades with which to fill them.

Ned was a plasterer by trade but his great passion was greyhound racing. He owned and trained dogs for years, spending as much time on their care and feeding as he did on his own. With little prospect of his modestly pedigreed squad winning the big money, the joy was in the contest itself, the camaraderie among the dog men and the knowledge that he'd done the very best job he could to prepare Crack Light, Quincy and the others for their moments in the arena.

He was a betting man, a dog man, a sportsman in that traditional sense evoked by the opening of 'The Plains of Kildare', the ballad that opens the great Andy Irvine/Paul Brady album from 1976: 'Come all you proud sportsmen and listen to my story, it's about gallant Stewball the gallant racing pony'.

When I rang my mother while covering the 2008 National Coursing Meeting in Clonmel, she told me Ned wanted to know how various trainers of his acquaintance were doing, and I passed on the info that evening. Next morning she walked the few yards between their houses and found him dead from a heart attack at the age of seventy-six.

Their brother Páraic shared Ned's sporting interests, though from an administrative rather than a competitive point of view. He'd been a member of Bord na gCon, and when I saw him at

Christmas Eve mass in Spiddal he was greatly looking forward to watching the holiday racing festival at Leopardstown with the *Racing Post* beside him.

The following year Páraic, who suffered from Parkinson's disease, took a very bad turn after being admitted to hospital in Galway. His family awaited the inevitable yet he rallied and after a few weeks returned home. The Feeneys were fighters, tempered by a tough but loving upbringing on a small farm whose land contained more stones than grass. They had three cows, two donkeys and three rooms in a thatched cottage for six children, two parents, an aunt and a grandmother.

It was the kind of Cois Fharraige existence captured in the great novels and short stories of the writer Máirtín Ó Cadhain, who came from one boreen over in Cnocán Glas. My mother, who remembers meeting him when she was a child, is particularly fond of 'The Road to Bright City', a story about a woman journeying from Spiddal to Galway to sell goods at the market, perhaps because she'd sold chickens in the city as a young girl herself.

Emigration was a regular feature of life: my grandmother had brothers in America and my mother's Aunt Peige who shared the house in Tuar Beag had been in service in New Zealand before returning home.

As a child I was fascinated, and a little intimidated, by my mother's Aunt Nora who worked as a maid for several decades in New York, sharing a flat in The Bronx after retiring with her sister Julia, where they listened to baseball on the radio in the evening and at night heard gunshots and saw the skies lit up by fires set in what had become one of the most dangerous urban areas in the world. They sent me a card for my First Communion. When Julia died Nora returned to live with my grandfather, New York having left her with an American accent – 'The cookies are in the closet, kids' – bionic hearing and nostalgic memories of dancing the Black Bottom.

She brought with her references from her employers which she kept in her bedroom until she died. From Carmel Wilson, daughter of Carmel Snow who'd been born in Dalkey and became editor of the American fashion magazine *Harper's Bazaar*. From Mrs Richard Ernst of Park Avenue, aka Susan Bloomingdale, whose grandfather had founded the prestigious New York store and whose father-in-law had been Harry Houdini's lawyer. From Evangeline Zalstem-Zalessky, daughter of one of three brothers who founded the Johnson & Johnson pharmaceutical company, one-time wife of the famous classical conductor Leopold Stokowski whom she divorced after he went on holidays to the Isle of Capri with Greta Garbo.

Evangeline, her obituary said, 'made the scene at all the best society functions'. I'm sure Aunt Nora's other employers did so too while she, and so many others like her, went unnoticed in the background as the plutocrats played. What autobiographies they left unwritten. What stories she could have told me about New York if ever I'd asked her.

Down that boreen on his way to America too came my grandfather's first cousin John Feeney, who'd end up running a saloon in Portland, Maine. His son, a college football star nicknamed Bull Feeney, became John Ford, the greatest film director of Hollywood's classic era. Returning to Ireland to make *The Quiet Man*, Ford visited his relations and expressed a desire to take some dilisk back to the States. My mother was dispatched to bring some in a jar to Lord Killanin's house where the director was staying. He rewarded her, in true Western style, with a fistful of dollars. Her sisters Maura and Bríd got parts as extras and my mother got to visit the set, where she watched John Wayne and Maureen O'Hara go through numerous takes of the scene where they shelter from a storm together. The scene provides the very useful service for an Irish person of extracting erotic potential from the act of getting drenched by the rain.

I walked up that same boreen with my mother and talked about the following day's match between Kilkenny and Galway. Not long ago we'd have gone to the game together but the reason it wouldn't happen now was the same reason her steps were shuffling and tentative like never before.

During the night of 22 August 2021, a few hours after engaging in our usual Sunday-evening phone dissection of the weekend's sporting action (the main topic being Limerick's overwhelming All-Ireland hurling final win over Cork), my mother suffered a stroke. My sister, who lives next door, found Mam lying

immobile on the floor the next morning. The ambulance took
her to University Hospital in Galway (she remembers two
very nice men whose optimism about Mayo's prospects in
the forthcoming football final proved ill-founded). My sister
phoned with the news and for the next couple of weeks I
dreaded every ring of the phone, imagining the news it might
bring.

Covid made things worse. I didn't see my mother for over
a year after its initial arrival. As a woman in her eighties who'd
survived two bouts of cancer, she was in the high-risk category.
We'd visited that summer when everyone had been vaccinated
and the pandemic was subsiding. Solving the mysteries of a
Galway escape room with her grandchildren, she seemed in
flying form. Yet the stroke was only a couple of months down
the line and by the time it happened Covid had returned with
a vengeance.

In a normal time my first instinct would have been to visit
her once she got out of hospital. But it wasn't possible and, the
stroke having badly affected her speech, I couldn't talk to her on
the phone either. Weeks of agonising limbo passed before we
managed a desultory conversation and I reassured my mother
that her halting, barely decipherable speech didn't sound that
different at all.

How strange those times seem now, just a few short years
ago yet somehow separated from the present by an enormous
gulf. I remember my mixture of excitement and trepidation at

the vaccination on 25 May at the Bantry Primary Care Centre, the military precision of the way we were processed and the numbers of people milling around lending a field hospital air to the proceedings. It was like a scene from some apocalyptic movie. So were a lot of things in those two shudder-inducing years. The whole thing seems vaguely unreal, like some odd drunken encounter hazily recalled the next morning through the shroud of last night's booze.

There was, for example, the weird attempt to blame the GAA for a sudden flare-up of Covid during the winter of 2020, people on social media attempting to prove it was all linked to county finals being played in front of minuscule crowds at the time. The GAA took its turn in the long line of national scapegoats.

Former president Liam O'Neill was just one of the people who urged the association to cancel the belated championships it had scheduled for November and December. I argued in my column that above all it was worth playing the championships for the sake of old people who'd been isolated by cocooning all year. The games would give them something to enjoy, talk about and look forward to during that grim and interminable pandemic winter.

I was thinking of my mother in particular. When the GAA decided to go ahead with the championships it meant a lot to her. She wasn't alone. These were championships unlike any other, the voices of the players echoing through the empty stadiums, but they were something to cling on to. Playing in that silence must have been an eerily unrewarding experience for the teams involved. Yet they did it all the same. There was a great selflessness about the enterprise which did the GAA enormous credit.

My mother and I discussed those games the same way we did those of previous championships. That was winter 2020 but twelve months later her stroke had sundered the normal conversational link between us. It felt as though we'd entered new territory.

Having opted against a visit the previous Christmas, we remained unsure about 2021. Covid, like Elton John, was making yet another comeback. On the morning of the proposed journey, myself, my three daughters and their mother took tests and watched them come up negative. In Charleville, where we always halt for grub and a stretch of the legs, we were still unsure about proceeding. As the dog pissed contemplatively against the side of a service station car wash we decided to press on. The familiar journey had never seemed such a trek.

When my mother opened the front door my first thought was that all the years had fallen upon her at once. Last time I'd seen her it was still hard to think of her as a woman in her eighties – now it was all too easy. She looked much smaller, her gait more stooped. Her indomitability in the face of cancer had become a family legend but there was an air of timidity and confusion about her. The moment felt like an unexpected encounter with a long-unseen acquaintance. The dominant emotion was a kind of embarrassment at our inability to find the words to express the changed reality which lay between us.

'You're looking well, Mam.'

'Thanks.'

In that moment, I was absolutely convinced this would be the last Christmas we'd spend together. Walking up the boreen in the dark a little later I thought of how beautiful she was and how easily she could be broken. I didn't cry but I swallowed very hard.

When my daughters returned to Cork I stayed up in Spiddal for a month to help my mother – who'd been staying with my sister since getting out of hospital – move back into her house. After making myself breakfast each morning I couldn't resist knocking on her bedroom door and asking, 'Are you alright, Mam?' After about a week of this she answered, 'Don't worry. I'm not dead.' I cut down the inquiries after that.

The American comedian Denis Leary once said there wasn't really a war going on in the North – all those explosions were just Irish men exploding with tension about their relationships with their fathers. Irish men's daddy issues have a venerable pedigree. It's there in James Joyce and John McGahern and

J.M. Synge and crossed the ocean to bedevil Eugene O'Neill and sundry other Irish American writers.

Yet most Irish men's primary parental relationship was probably with their mother. Especially for men my age and older, reared in an era where your father came in from work, flopped down in a chair, was handed a paper and given his dinner while wearing an invisible but highly effective 'Do Not Disturb' sign on his chest before heading off to the pub later that night to seek the company of other fathers who were, as my paternal grandmother observed, keen on combining the comforts of the married man's lot with the freedom of the bachelor's.

This blithely semi-detached attitude to fatherhood meant our mothers were what we had left. We weren't that keen on admitting the centrality of this relationship. The other one seems a bit more fitting. Better to mutter a few gruff stories about 'the oul fella' than run the risk of being labelled a 'mammy's boy', with all the sneaky homophobic connotations of that particular phrase.

The Irish mammy, like her Jewish and Italian counterparts, is often portrayed as an overwhelming larger-than-life figure. She needed to be. In a macho, harsh and sexist society which was a cold house for women and not exactly brimming with love for children either, the provision of affection and emotional solace was left almost entirely to the Irish mammy. They did a pretty great job in the circumstances.

My mother has gradually recovered from her stroke to the extent that someone who hadn't seen her for five years probably wouldn't notice much difference. But it took its toll on certain aspects of her life. She'll probably never drive again because getting insurance will require sitting the test again. Most of the things she'd read in the previous few years have been wiped from her memory. That's a shame because in her seventies she had become a voracious reader, making her way through the likes of Anne Tyler, Marilynne Robinson, Barbara Pym, Kent Haruf and, a particular favourite, Elizabeth Strout with the obsessive joy of someone making up for lost time.

She also doesn't feel able to go to big matches, so that Sunday I set out for Pearse Stadium alone to watch Kilkenny play Galway in a match which was expected to be a dress rehearsal for the Leinster final. Outside the gate I met Mullooly again. 'Boyle Sports have us seventh or eighth in the betting,' he informed me, 'but we're moving up slowly.' He looked much happier, like electioneering was growing on him.

What caught my eye that day was the discomfort of Henry Shefflin on the sideline. One of the three or four best players of all time, he'd chosen to manage Galway instead of waiting to possibly succeed Brian Cody as Kilkenny manager. His performance had been mixed: Galway had reached two All-

Ireland semi-finals and run the apparently invincible Limerick side close twice but they'd also suffered two Leinster final defeats against Kilkenny. 2024 felt like a defining year for him.

As a player Shefflin had radiated imperious self-assurance and seemed the personification of that Noreside sang-froid which had got his county out of so many close shaves. All traces of it had gradually vanished from his demeanour as a manager. That day in Galway he cut a tormented figure. By contrast Derek Lyng, his former team-mate who'd succeeded Cody a year after Shefflin crossed the Shannon, was calmness itself as he and his black-tracksuited cohorts patrolled the sideline with a proprietary air.

'Shut the fuck up, Henry,' shouted a Kilkenny fan behind me as Shefflin berated the ref. 'He's not even watching the match, he's so busy complaining.' Memories can be very short in the GAA. Not long ago he'd have proudly put Shefflin up on his shoulders.

It was an entertaining match which ended as a draw thanks to a last-gasp point by Galway's Conor Whelan. 'That feels like a win for us,' said the Galway woman sitting next to me who'd swapped memories of watching the GAA in London. I thought the opposite; Kilkenny had been short their two best forwards, Eoin Cody and Adrian Mullen, and their first-choice goalkeeper, Eoin Murphy, and Galway still couldn't beat them. You could see why Shefflin was worried.

I stayed in Spiddal with my mother and discussed the game. 'The ref gave everything against Galway,' she said, as she's said after every single game the county ever played. I hope I hear her say it a hundred more times. By midnight the Irish mammy and the mammy's boy had the game thoroughly dissected.

9

Playboys of the Western World

I STAYED ON IN GALWAY FOR THE FOLLOWING Sunday's Connacht football final between Galway and Mayo. Writing about the Connacht final in *The Road to Croker*, I couldn't suppress a certain triumphalism. After decades of poor-relation status, Connacht football was on the way up in 2003. Galway had won All-Irelands in 1998 and 2001 after Mayo had narrowly lost finals in 1996 and 1997. The west was wide awake. Where were the critics now?

Unfortunately Connacht hadn't won an All-Ireland since and its decades had been defined by Mayo's search for an All-Ireland, Irish sport's equivalent of the *Flying Dutchman's* eternal quest for a harbour in which to land.

In 1999, after the team which lost those 1996 and 1997 finals went down to Cork in the All-Ireland semi, an award-winning

71

Mayo novelist friend of mine said to me, as we watched a bunch of lads who looked like guards do the Macarena in Major Tom's, 'I don't think I can take much more of these disappointments.'

Much more? The torment was only starting. In the new millennium Mayo would reach eight finals and lose all of them, a run without precedent in football history. Their fans kept the faith and never stopped believing this year would be the one. They seemed the ultimate proof that the phrase 'it's better to travel hopefully than to arrive' was probably written by someone who'd arrived. Mayo fans began each season with the giddy excitement of kids heading for the beach before the reality of traffic jams, car sickness and feuding parents sets in along the way. There was a great majesty about this journey all the same. It had taken on the heroic proportions of an Irish search for the Holy Grail.

When Mayo won the 2023 league title in McStay's first season, even long-time sceptics suggested salvation might be at hand. Galway's runner-up slot and Roscommon's third place led to excitable talk of a western awakening and a first ever all-Connacht All-Ireland final. Instead Galway and Roscommon were beaten in the preliminary quarters and Mayo got hockeyed by Dublin one round later. Connacht would lie in slumber deep for a little while longer.

My provincial jingoism from 2003 proved sadly ill-founded but Mayo's exploits meant the Connacht final was no longer the dismal backwater spectacle of the eighties. Neither was Connacht, for that matter. A place once largely notable for economic underdevelopment, mass emigration and TDs you wouldn't trust to mind your coat without going through the pockets had become cool. A once depopulated landscape now swarmed with hipsters seeking to discover a profound connection with it. The west of Ireland was once more, as it had been back in the days when J.M. Synge listened to the conversation of Aran Islanders through the floor of the room in his lodgings, seen as a kind of Real Ireland. The spiritual, mystical, ethereal genuine article.

My native province does have a distinct identity. Cromwell said, 'To Hell or to Connacht,' not, 'To Hell or to Connacht and also those midlands counties which border Roscommon and maybe we can throw Cavan and Clare in too.' There's a sense of provincial belonging, though in my case, given that I haven't actually lived there for thirty-five years, it doesn't amount to much more than extreme irritation when I hear someone call it 'the wesht'.

The Connacht football final is Westfest. Even when played in Pearse Stadium, probably the most unloved of all major inter-county grounds. Older Galway fans still pine for Tuam.

Salthill, despite decades of championship games, still seems an interloper. The usual accretion of tradition through the passage of time just hasn't happened. Perhaps it's because, even on provincial final day, the town of Galway remains largely indifferent to the charms of the GAA. It has other things on its mind which it considers more interesting. Perhaps it's right. Between the Arts Festival, the Film Fleadh, the Races, the seaside and the general good vibes, Galway has enough going on already. It never seems consumed by the championship.

The city isn't exactly a GAA powerhouse. The spiritual homes of Galway football and hurling are located somewhere in the vicinities of Tuam and Loughrea respectively. City teams have won two county football titles and one hurling title in the past thirty years. Where Cork and Limerick are largely defined by sport, Galway's identity is centred around the arts. Michael D is their Roy Keane. On this fine Sunday people strolled along the Salthill prom in blissful ignorance of what was unfolding less than a mile away. This feeling of utter isolation from the business of the town contributes to Pearse Stadium's generally subdued atmosphere.

The prevailing prognosis was that Mayo were on the way up and Galway were on the way down. Having reached the All-Ireland final in 2022, Galway had never got going in 2023 and their season petered out with a loss to Mayo. 2024 hadn't been any more impressive; scraping past Sligo by a point in the semi added to the impression of manager Pádraic Joyce having done as much as he could with this team. Mayo's win over Galway in the league confirmed the impression of two teams heading in opposite directions.

About the only thing the two managers had in common was that they'd both been outstanding forwards. Mayo's Kevin McStay seemed the modern boss par excellence. An articulate analyst for RTÉ, he employed the same style in talking about his own teams, as though management were merely punditry by other means. McStay had actually been an army officer, reaching the rank of lieutenant colonel, but it was easy to imagine him heading up a tech company. There was a certain corporate sheen to his talk which was very impressive if you liked that kind of thing.

It wasn't all talk. The All-Ireland club title he'd won with St Brigid's and the Connacht championship he'd won with Roscommon were model achievements in making the very best of the material available. Mayo's persistent failure to appoint the Ballina man, considered a shoo-in for the job as far back as 2014 (McStay said he'd been the only man interviewed and still wasn't appointed), led to the county's fans regarding him as a kind of king over the water who'd have worked wonders if given the chance. His appointment in 2023 was accompanied by certain messianic expectations, never difficult to awaken in Mayo.

Whereas the Mayo man was a media darling, few managers had ever got less credit for steering a team to an All-Ireland final than Joyce in 2022.

This probably suited him fine. His obvious indifference to the media made it hard to imagine him on pundit duty. Pat

Comer's *A Season of Sundays*, a fly-on-the-wall look at the 1998 Galway team's unexpected march to the All-Ireland title, is the greatest ever GAA documentary. It always will be because it was the first of its kind. There's an unguardedness about the players' reactions which will never be there again.

Not everyone was unguarded. Towards the end of *A Season of Sundays* we get one brief shot of Joyce. He's sitting on the team bus with a wry smile on his face as if to say that the camera might have briefly captured him but that would be that. You've had your fun, that's all you're getting folks, move on. The same terseness informed his media relations as a manager. He had no interest in setting himself up as a guru of the game. This reluctance probably led to his being sorely under-estimated.

There was a wonderful polished plausibility about McStay. Even during Mayo's worst days the previous year, a surprise loss to Cork in the qualifiers, a heavy defeat by Dublin in the All-Ireland quarter-final, he could summon up convincing explanations for why this wasn't as bad as it seemed and might even be a necessary part of the plan.

Joyce on the other hand had an old-fashioned bluntness about him. No more able to hide his emotions than a committed supporter, he seemed crushed when Galway played badly, outraged when decisions went against them and enormously joyful when they won big games. The great loveliness of the photo of himself and his daughter embracing after the 2022

Connacht final win over Mayo is that neither seems aware of the crowd let alone the camera.

It seemed odd that McStay at sixty-one was fifteen years older than Joyce. The younger manager seemed more like someone from a past era, the old-school football man as opposed to the CEO-style coach. McStay was focused on executing a long-term project, Joyce was sending out a team to play football.

The first half in Salthill proved one of the season's turning points. Galway looked every inch a team which had scraped past Sligo. Mayo were faster, sharper and dominated possession by 65%–35%, a stat belonging more to a Manchester City match than one between these rivals. Galway were the classic example of a team there for the taking. They were reduced to trying to attack on the break like a European soccer team taking a pounding away from home.

Mayo didn't land the knockout punch. They didn't even attempt it. On several occasions one of their attackers, finding himself in a good scoring position, opted against taking the shot and turned away from goal to play the ball backwards or laterally. This happened so often it seemed as though the Mayo players had been instructed only to shoot from very specific areas. It felt like a policy decision. Their prevarication drove the visiting fans nuts and let the home team off the hook. For all their possession Mayo were only two up at the break and you sensed Galway drawing strength from the reprieve.

Mayo's over-elaboration was one of the things which had kept Galway in the game – the other was Damien Comer. Comer was that most beloved of GAA figures, the-forward-who-can-win-his-own-ball. Put any kind of delivery in his general direction and he'd make a good fist of getting it. He had the air and the strong jaw of a man who'd shoulder-charge a brick wall just for the hell of it. It was difficult to resist a smile of approval at the absolute whole-hearted determination with which he played the game. Comer, you felt, would have done pretty well in those roughhouse nineteenth-century variants, *caid* and the like, which preceded the invention of Gaelic football.

His supply was sporadic given Galway's paucity of possession but from half a dozen passes of varying quality he managed to score a brilliant long-range point, force a great save from the keeper, get fouled for a pointed free and set up another score.

The feeling there might be something in this game for Galway increased when they brought on Shane Walsh at half-time. Walsh was the opposite of Comer. He wasn't a win-your-own-ball kind of guy but the ultimate example of another archetype, the 'lovely footballer'.

David Clifford might have been the only forward with more natural ability. When it all clicked for Walsh, as it had in his bravura 2022 All-Ireland final performance, he was the Gaelic footballer as *objet d'art*. He kicked points from the most outrageous angles, went on blistering solo runs, made defenders look foolish by slowing down almost to a walk and then accelerating away from a standing start. They knew the trick was coming but couldn't do anything about it.

Yet if Walsh possessed an artist's gifts, he also had an artist's sensitivity. Sometimes he tightened up at the most crucial moments like a golfer getting the yips on the closing holes of a major. On other occasions his penchant for the spectacular and unexpected became a double-edged sword. When things didn't go right for him he looked much worse than a more conventional player would have done. Walsh himself admitted that he'd been 'stink' in 2023 and injury had limited his national league appearances. Yet his reappearance was a boost to Galway and a boon to neutrals. There was always the possibility of something special from Shane Walsh.

You could almost see the rust falling off his shoulders as he struggled to pick up the first ball which came his way. It should have been the most routine task for someone of Walsh's skill but he looked like he'd put the boots on the wrong feet. Yet he hustled and battled to win a free, which seemed to settle him down.

With eight minutes to go he hit a superb point to level the match, a minute later he struck another to put Galway one up. Walsh was feeling it and so were Galway but Mayo still seemed slightly the better team. Ryan O'Donoghue equalised, Matthew

Ruane put them ahead and with a minute of normal time left Tommy Conroy made it a two-point lead.

There were five minutes of injury-time. Galway pointed two frees to level things and with time almost up were awarded a third about fifty-five yards out. As a scoring opportunity, this was literally a long shot so Connor Gleeson was brought up to have a go, proceeding ceremoniously up the field as goalkeepers do in these circumstances.

Gleeson had his critics. For a big man he could seem oddly vulnerable under the high ball, as in the 2022 quarter-final against Armagh when his attitude to a series of long deliveries brought to mind Corporal Jones in *Dad's Army* running around waving his arms and shouting, 'Don't panic, Captain Mainwaring, don't panic.' He retained his place by virtue of a prodigiously long and accurate kick-out yet, as he shaped up to the last-gasp free a Galway doubter beside me declared, 'I've seen him hit these before. This could go fucking anywhere.'

It went over the bar. Mayo had time for one shot at an equaliser and kicked it wide. The final whistle brought an invasion of deliriously happy Galway supporters as Salthill did a passable impression of Tuam. A little disbelief may have been mixed in with the delight. The Tribesmen had won a game they never looked like winning until they actually won it. The home team hadn't been great and Mayo had thrown the game away to a degree, but the mysterious workings of momentum engendered a feeling that Galway might go a long way on the back of this. It proved correct.

Back in Spiddal my mother was ecstatic although convinced that David Gough, who'd awarded her home county three borderline frees in injury-time, had displayed the unforgivable anti-Galway bias general among referees. We'd been brought up on tales of the great Galway teams of her younger days. There was the 1956 All-Ireland-winning team which featured the Terrible Twins, Seán Purcell and Frank Stockwell, and the three-in-a-row-winning side of 1964–6. Martin Newell, Mattie McDonagh, John Donnellan, Enda Colleran and Noel Tierney came in for special praise there, but the one player who overtopped everyone else in her personal pantheon was Pat, always called Pateen, Donnellan. When a few years back I received a kind letter from him it was one of the highlights of my journalistic career. He'd enjoyed such legendary status in my childhood it was like getting a phone call from Cúchulainn.

My mother and a friend from Kerry who worked with her in the civil service spent many happy days in Croke Park during the sixties. Galway weren't always involved and there were players from other counties with a special place in her affections: Offaly's Greg Hughes, Gerry O'Malley of Roscommon, Mick O'Connell.

Her own mother, Mamo as we knew her, had been so passionately involved with Galway's fortunes that when a radio broadcast revealed an impending close finish she'd walk up the boreen, wait till she knew the game was over and walk back to the house to discover their fate. In the seventies she was still listening to matches on *Sunday Sport* on a small radio of such magnificent crackliness it took a while to work out who was playing never mind what the score was. She'd have loved Galway's injury-time resurrection.

The day before the Connacht final I'd gone to Pat Collins' film of John McGahern's novel *That They May Face the Rising Sun* in the Palas Cinema. McGahern didn't just diverge from the romantic notion of the 'soulful west', his work was an antidote to it. The flinty, watchful and unsentimental nature of his characters probably struck a chord with me because I knew the physical and emotional territory. Cootehall, where McGahern had been brought up in the eponymous barracks of his debut novel, was just six miles from Boyle where I went to secondary school, had my first job and wolfed down curry chips on wintry evenings in the shadow of the limestone clock tower at the top of the town before thumbing home after watching a movie in the Crescent Cinema, going to a disco in the Royal Hotel or being turned away from the one in Parkers Nightclub.

His books were a revelation. This was how people round

me spoke, in a kind of glancing fashion so that an awful lot was hidden underneath the words in a subtext only another local could discern. It was how they reacted to things, lived their lives, viewed the world, but until then I'd never imagined it could be the stuff of literature.

I'm not sure McGahern was much of a GAA fan, though there's a very astute observation in his story 'Eddie Mac' about how as the titular football hero gets slower with age the cleverness in his game begins to look like cowardice to the supporters. That the disgraced title character in 'The Creamery Manager' looks back on a day at the Ulster football final in Clones as a moment of perfect happiness shows that McGahern knew how emotionally important the GAA could be to people.

I knew Pat fairly well. He'd made a documentary on McGahern in 2005, they'd got on well and I suspected he felt under particular pressure to do the greatest possible justice to the book. So I sat down in that Galway cinema feeling the nerves of a fan waiting for his team to take the field.

There was nothing to worry about. *That They May Face the Rising Sun* was the best Irish film I'd seen in years. There were small moments in it – Lalor Roddy as Patrick fighting desperately the rising urge to take offence and cause a scene while knowing he'd fail because there was that awkward streak in him, Sean McGinley's character's panic-stricken appeal to his neighbour, 'You wouldn't leave me,' when he thought he'd been abandoned in the pub, the dammed-up desolation of a man alone bursting suddenly and helplessly forth – which made you gasp from the truth of them.

The movie perfectly captured the spirit of the writer and the book but it also bore Pat's own stamp. The characters seemed kinder because he was a gentler and more forgiving artist. McGahern's characters, like their native province, were more in the forwards-who-can-win-their-own-ball than the 'lovely footballers' line. This was a look at their world from a slightly different angle and I thought the novelist might have approved. He had an austere reputation and his posthumously published letters revealed a waspish side in tune with the milieu he sprang from. But he had been very kind and friendly to my father when both were undergoing cancer treatment and knew they were for the high jump.

The film and the book captured the dailiness of our daily lives, the way they mainly meander on without epiphany or catharsis and the strange hard-won beauty in that. Reviewers described it as a portrait of a bygone era (it was set in the seventies), but it seemed to me that underneath the surface the essential rhythm of rural life hadn't changed that much. The GAA with all those Connacht finals succeeding one another year after year was part of its great slowly unwinding song. That reassuring consistency was a great part of its appeal.

As I took the bus from Spiddal to Galway the morning after the final a passenger asked the driver if he'd gone to the match.

'I did in me shite. Pick the best fifteen from the two of them and they wouldn't beat Dublin.'

There was a bit of the true spirit of the west in that too.

10

Saturday Night Fervour

CORK'S VICTORY OVER LIMERICK IN PÁIRC UÍ Chaoimh was the moment the 2024 hurling championship caught fire. Everything was different after that.

None of the home fans streaming into the city that Saturday evening thought they'd be doing anything other than saying goodbye to their hopes for another year. Limerick were probably the greatest team in history, odds-on favourites to provide concrete proof of that status by becoming hurling's first five-in-a-row All-Ireland winners. The trouncing they'd given Tipperary in their last match suggested a keener appetite than ever.

They hadn't been as impressive in their opener against Clare but their ability to turn a nine-point deficit entering the final quarter into a three-point victory burnished their aura of invincibility still further. Limerick would always find a way to win.

Cork by contrast had become the team which always found a way to lose when it mattered most. Their fans had actually entered 2024 in an unusually optimistic mood. The Rebels were undeniably unlucky the previous year when only two single-point defeats prevented their qualification from the Munster round robin. Their new manager, Pat Ryan, had steered the county to an All-Ireland under-20 title in 2020, which had been the county's first in twenty-two years, and then made it two in a row. In 2021 a first minor crown in twenty years added to the impression of a county on the way back.

Yet their first two matches, narrow defeats by Waterford and Clare, suggested nothing had changed after all. Defeat by Limerick would send Cork out early once again. How had it come to this for the GAA's most successful county? When as a kid I read about the All-Ireland famine Cork endured between 1954 and 1966 it seemed incredibly strange to me. Cork were winners, the county's famous self-confidence based to a large extent on their hurling victories. When they sought a hat-trick of All-Irelands in the 2006 final they were looking to do something no team had done in twenty-eight years. The previous three-in-a-row winners had also been Cork. As had been the ones before that in 1952, 1953 and 1954.

That 2006 final was hurling's equivalent of one of those

battles – the Greeks beating the Persians at Marathon, Attila the Hun getting turned back at Châlons-sur-Marne – which change the course of history. Kilkenny, who'd gone in as outsiders, went on to win nine All-Irelands in eleven years. Cork hadn't won one since. The fallow spell encompassed eighteen years and counting. A bitter players' strike had destroyed the idea of a superior Cork way of doing things. Even after the dust settled, a climate of disillusion and mistrust pervaded relations between ordinary GAA members and the county board. Now the old guard had been ousted off the pitch but ultimate triumph seemed as far away as ever.

Cork's most recent All-Ireland final appearance in 2021 saw them ship a sixteen-point beating from a Limerick team posting an all-time record total for a decider, despite cruising through most of the second half. Most of the same players would be involved in what looked likely to be Cork's last stand. Maybe Pat Ryan's too. There was speculation he might be replaced by Ben O'Connor who'd been in charge of the previous year's All-Ireland under-20-winning team and would be the twelfth manager since 2000 if appointed.

There was a giddy good humour about the crowd that night. One gang of supporters was convinced they couldn't lose, the other was sure they'd nothing left to lose. A massive merry mosaic of intermingled red and green jerseys overflowed from Goldbergs bar on the docks, the last pit stop before the long walk out the marina. The achievement represented by the contract of goodwill that enables scenes like this shouldn't be under-estimated. Much is made of the absence of crowd trouble at GAA matches which means fans don't have to be separated. The ability of fans to by and large socialise together without incident seems even more remarkable. There is a lot of drink involved, trouble is not unknown in Cork or Limerick city, and there are certainly lads around who fall under the old heading of 'tasty enough clients'. Yet the communal carnival rolls on in a way that would be unthinkable in the vicinity of an English soccer match or even at some League of Ireland games with much smaller crowds. GAA hooliganism just isn't a thing. You'd be embarrassed to try it. The only hassle caused was to a cop on traffic duty appealing 'Ah lads keep off the road', to limited effect.

Even the young women merrily singing 'We are red, we are white, we are fucking dynamite. With a nick nack Paddy whack give the dog a bone, why don't Limerick fuck off home' seemed so obviously inspired by mischief rather than malice it was hard to imagine anyone taking offence. Eighteen years of hurt had not dimmed the enthusiasm of the game's noisiest and most colourful supporters. Later that night a taxi driver told me he'd brought one of the 'hats, flags, scarves and headbands' sellers to the Dublin train. 'There's nobody like Cork,' said your man, 'I brought two hundred Cork hats and I sold all of them. I brought fifty Limerick hats and I'm going home with forty.'

As the sound of some Irish tenor warbling 'Step it out Mary my fine daughter, show your legs to the countryman' died away on the public address system, I fell into conversation with a guy from Midleton who said he was seventy, looked a decade younger and reminisced about his club breaking the stranglehold of the city giants Blackrock, St Finbarr's and Glen Rovers on the Cork senior title in 1983. He told me a key player on that team was in very bad health these days. He'd just seen him being wheeled into the game.

When I told him I was from Sligo he recalled seeing Leonard Cohen playing at Lisasdell House. My west Cork connection prompted him to mention Michelin stars earned by the Customs House in Baltimore and the Chestnut in Ballydehob. Had I eaten in either of them? No, but I used to buy sausages in Skibbereen Market from Frank Krawczyk whose son Robbie was the main man in the Chestnut.

As we killed the time before the throw-in together I realised how much I'd missed these easy Irish conversations between strangers with their search for connection and an angle which sets the ball rolling. It was a small but significant pleasure after the isolation of Covid and self-imposed quarantine of the succeeding years.

The loyalty of Cork's fans meant I could only get a terrace ticket at the City End. It was a long time since I'd watched a game from behind the goal. Years in the press box convince you a spot near the half-way line is the best place for an overall view of what's going on.

Watching from behind the goal lends a particular intensity to the viewing experience all the same. There's a visceral joy in seeing the ball rattle the net just in front of you, a feeling you've been granted privileged access, an intimate knowledge of the goal denied to the crowd cheering in the stands. On the other hand, action down the other end can seem like a rumour from another land – the ball you thought was heading for the net turning out on subsequent TV viewing to have been blocked thirty yards out.

Being behind the Limerick goal in the first half that night offered a front-row seat at the unlikeliest of spectacles. For thirty-five minutes Cork destroyed Limerick and did so largely by the simplest means possible.

It had seemed that Cork's theoretical, if improbable, path to victory would involve keeping the ball wide and using their pace to stretch the Limerick defence. Limerick's backs weren't slow but they were less quick than they were strong. The one Cork tactic guaranteed to fail was pucking the ball long at the centre of a physically powerful and aerially dominating Limerick defence. Route one would bring zero rewards.

Yet here was Cork keeper Patrick Collins launching puck-outs into the heart of a Limerick defence reduced to a state of panic by this most basic of gambits. Collins pucked the ball out, Brian Hayes broke it down to Shane Barrett who put Séamus Harnedy in for Cork's first goal. And when Séamus Flanagan's goal for Limerick suggested normal service would soon be resumed, Collins went long again, Harnedy caught the ball and passed it to Barrett who stuck it in the back of the net.

The nature of those goals added to a general impression of unreality. Cork led by eight points at half-time but it could have been much more, Nickie Quaid having made fantastic saves from Hayes and Barrett.

It was like a dream. Limerick's half-back line had squeezed the life out of Cork in the past but Diarmaid Byrnes and Declan Hannon, normally paragons of consistency, were being run ragged by Harnedy and Barrett. The third member of that unit had difficulties of another sort. Kyle Hayes and Gearóid Hegarty were the two players who personified the fearsome nature of this Limerick team. They were huge men – Hayes was six foot five and Hegarty was six four – who married considerable skill with a ferocious physical intensity that saw them singled out as villain figures by opposition supporters. Neither was a hatchet man but the sheer amount of room they needed to manoeuvre sometimes resulted in opponents shipping eye-catching knocks.

Hegarty began as a dual player whose physical gifts out-weighed his technical ones as a hurler. His progress had been remarkable so that now there was a beautiful incongruity about such a big man possessing such delicacy of touch.

Hayes had been earmarked for stardom early on. He'd made his senior debut at the age of eighteen and scored four points from play in Limerick's 2018 All-Ireland final win over Galway when just twenty. The only question mark over him concerned deployment. Centre half-forward in 2018, he'd switched to wing-back but had also been tried at full-forward. He'd probably have done well in any position on the field.

There were few more spectacular sights in hurling than Hayes surging forward from the Limerick half-back line. One such surge had ended with a magnificent individual goal in the 2021 Munster final against Tipperary. A frisson ran through the crowd every time Hayes moved forward. He was so big, so quick and so determined it took multiple defenders to stop him. Quite a few of those runs ended with a Hayes point or one created for a team-mate. These forays exuded so much menace you could almost hear the theme from *Jaws* playing in the background.

Yet he too seemed subdued that night even before a tussle with Declan Dalton left him stretched on the ground just before half-time. What exactly transpired remains a mystery. Before the season ended I would meet a Limerick man who swore he'd seen Dalton deliver 'a rap in the balls' to Hayes and a Cork man who insisted Hayes had hit the deck without any contact being made at all. Both swore the incident had happened just in front of them and they'd had a perfect view of it.

The sight of Hayes prone on the ground probably boosted Cork's morale further because one knock against the team was that it was 'too nice', a particular problem against such uncompromising opposition as Limerick. If Dalton had felled Hayes, it seemed proof of a new ruthlessness in Cork. There was probably as much talk about Dalton's alleged deed afterwards as about Barrett and Harnedy's goals. Players who did this kind of thing were praised for 'setting down a marker'. This might sound like primitive law of the jungle stuff but a lot of fans believed in it, and so did a lot of players.

It was all grist to Cork's mill but mingled with the delight and the disbelief was anticipation of a second-half Limerick riposte. It was a bit like the feeling you get waiting for a 'red warning' storm to show up.

Like Ophelia, the Limerick backlash arrived on schedule. Hegarty led the way, laying on a second goal when a Collins short puck-out left Seán O'Donoghue facing a physical contest with him. It was the greatest mismatch since Tina Reynolds took on Abba in the 1974 Eurovision Song Contest. Hegarty cast the corner-back aside and set up Flanagan for a goal. Limerick were just two points down with half of the second period left.

A few minutes later Hegarty swooped on a loose ball thirty yards out. From behind the goal the impression of sheer physical power was extraordinary. As he burst through three Cork defenders, you almost expected him to keep going, leap on to the terrace and go through the back wall. He slipped a pass to Flanagan who did something which has stuck in my mind, as random moments do over the course of a championship.

With the sliotar heading towards him, Flanagan took a couple of quick steps away from goal before catching and driving it home from a tricky angle almost without looking. There was something beautifully instinctive about those couple of steps which took him away from Collins and about his knowledge of where the goal was. It was a hat-trick for the full-forward, a player I'd always admired because of the barnstorming gusto with which he played the game. All his goals were dispatched with a sweep and a flourish. His typical point seemed to be a first-time shot executed while off-balance and under pressure near the sideline. He didn't really do routine scores.

Cork didn't collapse, but when they trailed by four points with four minutes left you could sense their fans beginning to compose little consolatory notes to themselves. The Rebels had been brilliant in the first half, they hadn't let themselves down, there was no disgrace losing to a Limerick team playing like this, the performance gave great hope for the future. All of these things were true but deep down the fans knew they wouldn't matter one jot when they left the ground facing a long, empty summer for the second successive year.

Then an odd thing happened. Cork hit a point and another point and then another point. You'd have expected Limerick to punch home their advantage as they normally did but there was just one in it with a couple of minutes of injury-time left. The home fans weren't exactly buzzing with anticipation. Limerick's expertise in tight finishes was such you presumed they'd close it out. Or, agony of agonies, Cork would get a draw which would be both a fine achievement and absolutely no use at all because they'd still be out. It was Shane Kingston time. Kingston was hurling's little girl with the curl in the middle of her forehead. When he was good he was really really good but when he was bad he was horrid. On the really really good days this guy with his blistering speed and eye for a score looked completely unmarkable. On the horrid days his first touch would go awry and it would be downhill from there. The exciting thing about Kingston was that the opposition didn't know where his solo runs were going. The drawback was that sometimes he didn't seem sure himself.

That lack of consistency was why he'd only come on as a sub. But here was the solo run to beat them all. Picking up the ball in his own half, Kingston went at the heart of the Limerick defence, travelling at pace, moving further and further into the distance for those of us with old-man eyesight behind the far goal. Defenders closed in on him and you dreaded the moment of dispossession but he kept going. Suddenly there was a huge furore at the other end. As though we were watching an overseas game with a delay in the satellite signal, the electrifying realisation that referee Seán Stack had awarded a penalty took a second to travel to us.

I expressed puzzlement as to how it could be a penalty as Kingston, even allowing for the distorting effect of distance, didn't seem to be near the square when Hayes, as though performing a personal tribute to Limerick's other favourite sport, executed a rugby tackle. My Leonard Cohen-loving neighbour explained that deliberate fouls on players with goalscoring opportunities were punished by a penalty. It had been so long since I'd seen the punishment applied that I'd completely forgotten it.

It was a huge call by Dublin referee Seán Stack. He was entirely correct but the easy option was to just award a free in. There wouldn't have been any great controversy if he did. The teams would have been level and everyone had got used to the professional foul rule being honoured more in the breach than the observance. But he had the courage to do the right thing and changed the course of the hurling championship by doing so.

Pat Horgan lined up the penalty. This was his seventeenth year on the Cork senior team. At no other point in history could a player have played so long for the county without winning an All-Ireland but this was how it had worked out for the Glen Rovers man. Only two players in championship history had totalled more than 500 points. By the end Horgan would lead T.J. Reid on the all-time list by 629 to 604 despite having played six games fewer. It was one of the great hurling careers but when you'd played as long as Horgan had every season now began with speculation that it might be your last. If he missed this penalty Cork would be out of the championship and he might not play another home game for the county. It was hard to imagine a less fitting final act. That he was facing the best goalkeeper in the game added to the tension.

Yet greatness has its privileges. Horgan put the shot away with the emphatic coolness of a player practising penalties at training. Cork were one up with seconds left. Limerick's invincibility loomed large but Cork won a free in their next attack. Horgan came out to try a long-range free but the risk of a counter-attack should it fall short meant Ryan told him to puck it down the wing. It was the kind of decision a manager would never be forgiven for if it went wrong. Horgan obeyed orders and sent the ball down to Brian Hayes in the right corner.

Hayes was a physical prodigy to match his namesake Kyle but there was a coltish quality about him as if at twenty-two he hadn't fully grown into his frame. With time running out, the safest thing was probably to run the ball down into the corner and seek a free. Instead Hayes took on his man, made space and struck a point which seemed like an exclamation mark at the end of an extraordinary tale. The final whistle went from the puck-out and Cork fans invaded the pitch with the special South American-style fervour reserved for victories nobody saw coming.

It was, despite my compromised viewing position, the most satisfying match I'd ever been at in my life. Other great games lay ahead but there was something unique about Cork–Limerick part one. Perhaps because it never let up. Even classic games contain some brief lull but there was none that night.

Cork went at Limerick hammer and tongs in the first half and Limerick retaliated with all guns blazing in the second. There was no time to catch your breath or take stock. All you could do was allow yourself to be swept along by the flow. It was like one of those turbulent plane journeys where things never level off sufficiently to catch your bearings.

The lull should logically have come when Limerick led by four points with four minutes left. The champions would normally have relaxed, played with freedom and seen it out from there. But Cork kept coming and Kingston's run, courageous, absurdly optimistic and ultimately irresistible, summed up the spirit which got them home.

11

Hozier Live in Thurles

CORK–LIMERICK HAD BEEN ONE OF THE GREATEST games in championship history but unfortunately most GAA fans hadn't seen it, something which brought the controversy over the GAAGO streaming service to a head. There was no subject I heard discussed more often on my travels. Discussed might be the wrong word because every conversation I heard about GAAGO involved people agreeing with each other about how much they disliked it. Not once did I hear someone bring up any of the points advanced by its media defenders: that the price was reasonable, that the GAA were entitled to make money from streaming their games and that it enabled the showing of matches which otherwise wouldn't have been televised at all.

I agreed with GAAGO's critics but the virtual unanimity and strength of the opposition slightly puzzled me. Why did it get people's goat to such an extent?

This hadn't been the first Munster championship match consigned to GAAGO; all three of Cork's games to date had been exiled there. The previous year a furore had been sparked by the hiving off of another Cork game, a home match against Tipperary, which also turned out to be a classic and in normal circumstances would have been a no-brainer for RTÉ to broadcast.

The thing was that in the season's opening months the Munster hurling championship and to a lesser extent its Leinster counterpart were the only show in town. The football championship's convoluted structure had rendered its provincial competitions meaningless. All the moderately strong teams had already qualified for the latter stages of the championship by virtue of their league placings.

Given that they'd then play twenty-four games to bring the number of remaining teams down from sixteen to twelve, you could argue that the football championship wouldn't start in earnest until 22 June, four weeks after the Munster hurling round robin had ended. The Munster competition brought together five strong teams who were so evenly matched that six of the ten round robin games were decided by three points or less and another was a draw. Almost every game mattered a great deal and was played with an intensity which reflected that.

No football game in May mattered and they were contested accordingly.

Given that the biggest and most meaningful games usually end up on TV, you'd have expected the national broadcaster to show as many Munster hurling matches as possible.

The fact that this didn't happen led fans to the conclusion that the huge popular appeal of Munster games meant it was being used to drive subscriptions to GAAGO. Cork were being used as a cash cow. You could argue about the ethics of this. You could make a case for it being a cunning commercial strategy. What you couldn't do was deny it was happening.

But that was what the GAA hierarchy in Croke Park and their apologists attempted to do. They spoke about having a responsibility to broadcast games in other provinces, even if they didn't mean anything. They suggested maybe Cork hurlers weren't that big a deal anymore. They even tried to foment a phoney war between hurling and football fans by painting the former as purists with a lack of respect for the latter.

The truth was that a game like Cork–Limerick's appeal didn't stop with imaginary hurling fundamentalists and also didn't stop at the provincial boundaries of Munster. Everyone knew it had been exiled to GAAGO for financial reasons but had to endure being told that other considerations were responsible.

A couple of months later, almost Jarlath Burns' first action as the new president of the GAA was to mount a passionate defence of GAAGO during which he admitted that of course they'd kept back some big games to drive subscriptions because that was the way of the world. Everyone knew this already and had passed no heed on the people telling them otherwise. But the specious justifications added another little drop to the store of national cynicism. The other problem with GAAGO's public image was its being a 50:50 partnership between the GAA and RTÉ. Conflicts of interest didn't come much clearer than that. The more money GAAGO made, the more money RTÉ made, so the broadcaster had a vested interest in keeping some big matches off its main channels. This was happening at a time when the station, after the revelations of Ryan Tubridy's financial arrangements sent all kinds of dominoes toppling, was in very bad odour with the public.

In an effort to regain the affection of its licence-payers, and of the politicians who could provide the money to keep it in the style to which it had become accustomed, RTÉ had been making high-minded noises about the importance of public service broadcasting. Yet the GAAGO lash-up revealed their old habit of acting like a private commercial entity when it suited. You had to believe that when the GAA furnished RTÉ with the list of proposed TV fixtures the RTÉ people who served on the GAAGO board suddenly changed from the GAA's confederates to its adversaries while trying to negotiate a better deal for the viewers.

If you do believe that, I can get you a fantastic deal on the swing bridge in Portumna. Maybe the biggest problem with

RTÉ's involvement in GAAGO was not that it was unethical but that it insulted everyone's intelligence. By the end of the season the Competition Authority, who'd never got round to clearing the arrangement, were apparently making noises that prompted the GAA to put a package of several matches out to open tender.

Most defences of GAAGO proceeded on the basis that the GAA would always need money and was entitled to make as much as possible from its matches. Those making this point presented the desire to extract the maximum return from every transaction as a kind of immutable scientific law. It's not. It's the product of a political ideology expounded by the likes of Margaret Thatcher whose great achievement, a critic once observed, was to put a price tag on everything.

Nothing in Irish life opposes this grimly utilitarian view of existence more effectively than the workings of the GAA itself at grass roots level. The entire edifice is built on volunteer effort. If people were to consider what they put into their local clubs on the basis of financial benefit it wouldn't be worth it. None of them think like that.

The GAA is our greatest rebuke to the idea that money is what matters most in life, an idea which has resulted in the odious rack-renting which makes so many people's lives a misery, dynamic pricing by hotels any time a big event comes to town and a general 'rip-off Republic' mentality. So it was very odd to see the association's interests being defended in these 'live in the real world, baby, and look at the bottom line' gombeen man terms.

GAAGO was like the infamous proposed water charges of blessed memory. There was no point lecturing people about the necessity to pay or deriding their opposition as 'populist'. They just didn't like the idea. There was no point telling them how reasonable the price was because they suspected, as with the water charges, that once the principle was accepted nothing could prevent the price being jacked up in the future.

Another objection to GAAGO was that old people would find it difficult to set it up online. This resulted in some amusing fake outrage of the 'Are you insulting the old people of this country by disparaging their computer skills?' variety. But some poor unfortunates do find this kind of thing difficult.

On the night of the Laois–Offaly game in Portlaoise I discovered you required a pre-booked ticket. Except for one turnstile that took cash but not cards. 'You may buy the ticket online, or get one in SuperValu,' suggested its operator. I got the Ticketmaster site on my phone. They weren't selling these tickets. I had to go to a GAA website and set up an account there. That sounded easy enough but technical incompetence prevented me keeping two windows open simultaneously. I kept leaving the site and having to start again. *Create new password.* Did I have an old one? *You will need to add another credit card.* Another? Locked out again. Brilliant. *You have two minutes and thirteen seconds remaining.* The pressure was on.

Log in. I thought I had logged in. What in the name of God is Google Go? I gave up, walked round the corner to SuperValu and missed the first ten minutes of the match.

When I was writing about older people who'd struggle to access GAAGO I pictured some oul lad living up the side of a mountain with more hair in his ears than on his head. But standing defeated outside O'Moore Park I realised that I was the older-generation-who-have-trouble-with-technology. My follicular head-to-ears ratio wasn't great either.

Further technological problems arrived the next Sunday when I tried to get my pre-booked ticket for the train to Thurles at Kent Station. The machine refused to co-operate and after several tries I realised I'd actually booked passage for the following Sunday. With the train sold out and Thurles inaccessible by bus from Cork, things looked momentarily bleak. An Iarnród Éireann staff member came over to ask me if I was OK and I explained the problem.

'Just get on the train and find a spot. They're not going to stick to the pre-booked seats on this one anyway.'

My carriage was packed with immensely excited Cork lads in their twenties wearing county jerseys. Just one win had reawakened that feeling of embarking on a glorious quest. The amazing trademark confidence had returned as well. Things had been the same when I wrote the first book but the survival of this spirit seemed remarkable given that Cork hadn't even made a Munster final since 2018.

It would have seemed like a nightmare scenario for me not long ago and a definite trigger for my travel anxiety. Yet, though there were a few butterflies, it never crossed my mind to leave the train. My confidence was growing with every week and every journey. I didn't feel impregnable or entirely relaxed but the feeling of ordeal seemed to be gradually diminishing.

As the cans were cracked open and the singing began, the train had the air of a boisterous pub on wheels. Suddenly everyone noticed the presence of an interloper. At one end of the carriage stood a man on his own, late thirties, long-haired, suntanned and bearded, in a Tipperary jersey. You could sense the communal hackles going up even before the chants of 'What do we think of Tipp? Shit' and suggestions that Tipp fuck off home. Your man didn't turn a hair. Next thing all the Cork fans started pointing at him and singing with great glee about being too sweet for me.

This puzzled me. Was it some new football chant containing a deadly veiled insult? I googled the words and found they were the chorus of a song by … 'Hozier, Hozier, give us a wave. Hozier, give us a wave.'

He didn't look exactly like Hozier but he looked enough like him. When I told them about it later, my daughters were amused that I didn't know that song. Several times that summer I'd ask them if they'd heard some song only to discover I was probably the only one in the country who hadn't. Such are the penalties of reclusion. The Cork fans sang 'Take Me to

Church' before doing 'Too Sweet' again. Their target continued to display the cool nerve of a man in an old Hamlet cigar ad.

'Hozier, Hozier, give us a song. Come on, Hozier. Give us a song.'

So he did. 'Dirty Old Town'. He had a fine voice and the Cork fans roared along with him, adding a verse celebrating Liverpool centre-back Virgil van Dijk before cheering and clapping like we were already at the game. They did a few of their own songs, 'Oh to be a, oh to be a rebel', and one I hadn't heard before, 'Eoin, Eoin Eoin, Eoin Eoin, Eoin Eoin Downey', followed by 'Robert, Robert Robert, Robert Robert, Robert Robert Downey', to the tune of 'No Limit' by 2 Unlimited. But deep down they knew what they really wanted.

'Hozier, Hozier, give us a song. Another song, Hozier.'

'As I was going over the Cork and Kerry mountains, I met with Captain Farrell and his money he was counting.'

This sent the audience into a frenzy altogether. Guys were standing on the seats and beating the ceiling so hard I was amazed nothing broke or fell down. The abandon was so general you could forget that this wasn't just a hurling train but also an ordinary passenger service. A young American couple were looking at the carry-on in amazement. God knows what they made of it.

From then on every time the Rebel brigade launched into an abusive chant about Tipp, one of them would shout, 'But not Hozier. Not you, Hozier.'

As the train pulled into Thurles, the hero of the hour finally spoke rather than sang. 'Welcome, boys, to the home of hurling.'

As the Cork fans filed down to the end of the carriage, they all stopped to shake hands with Hozier, who accepted this homage like a king acknowledging the tribute of his courtiers. He was one of the coolest men I'd ever seen.

Outside Semple Stadium the European electioneering continued. A man stood on a platform shouting that the Irish people wouldn't take this anymore and gesticulating furiously. He looked like Basil Fawlty losing the head with a group of German tourists. Two sidekicks flanked him at ground level beside a sign which told me this was the Irish National Party.

Meanwhile Seán Kelly was standing quietly as a long line of people queued up to shake his hand. 'The wife would have killed me if I didn't,' said one guy. Kelly was an unlikely politician, being about the least flamboyant and charismatic Kerryman who'd ever lived. Yet people really liked him and respected above all the role he'd played in 2005 as GAA president in changing the rulebook so soccer and rugby could be played in Croke Park.

On the day of the vote at GAA Congress most people believed Kelly and his allies wouldn't get the necessary two-thirds majority. He had the undoubted support of the association's grass roots members but that support rested on delegates who generally erred on the side of caution. Just before the vote was taken an Ulster official gave a speech disparaging those who sought change. It was the performance of someone who was sure he was on the winning side and wanted to rub it in to the president personally. Kelly had to sit there and take it but had the last laugh when the vote was taken. The vote for change forever altered the perception of the GAA in Irish society as a whole. In voting for inclusivity, generosity and modernity it had destroyed an unfair caricature of the association as hidebound, conservative and insular, which would have been given credence by a 'no' vote. People still remembered Kelly's determination to do the right thing. It was no surprise when he got more votes than anyone else in the country on election day.

About to go into the stadium, I noticed Cork fans streaming down a passage to where a large crowd was gathered in front of a TV screen. Clare's match against Waterford was nearing the end. Whatever happened against Tipperary, Cork would almost certainly be eliminated if Waterford won or drew this game. No one had given this much thought because the presumption was that a Clare team good enough to beat Cork away would manage Waterford at home easily enough. The Banner had led by five points at half-time, were three up with injury-time running out and as I came in one of their forwards was in a perfect position to land the insurance point.

He missed it and Waterford swept up the field to win a penalty, which Stephen Bennett put away. The teams were level and with a minute left Cork were going out. Shock gripped the Cork fans. After all the excitement on the way to Thurles, were Cork going to be out before the game even started? Clare won a long-range free. Hurray. But it was drifting unmistakably wide. Nooooo. Defenders and forwards converged on the ball and it went over the end-line. Were the officials awarding a puck-out? The whistle would blow while it was in the air and that'd be curtains for Cork. Hang on, they were having second thoughts. It was a 65. Waterford manager Davy Fitzgerald was losing it on the sideline and Cork's fate was in the hands of Mark Rodgers. He landed the 65 and the place rang with relieved cheers. There'd be a meaningful game to watch after all. At least the Rebels wouldn't be knocked out by events elsewhere.

Tipperary had been even worse in their first two games than Cork, scraping a draw with Waterford in injury-time and getting trounced by Limerick, so the expectation was that they'd put a monumental effort into this one. It certainly looked like that when Mark Kehoe scored a goal for them after just twenty seconds. Cork recovered pretty quickly and the teams were level or close to it for the rest of the half. However there was a significant difference between the way the teams were scoring. A lot of Tipp's scores were superb strikes from out on the wing or fine solo efforts, the kind it was difficult to replicate for a full match. Cork's came easier, their forwards had their men beaten for pace and some of the points could have turned into goal chances had the scorer taken a few more steps.

This sounds like a pretty perspicacious analysis given how the match turned out but I might not actually have believed it. I came up with it to console the man beside me, a chubby little middle-aged guy from Cork city in a state of extreme agitation. Every Tipp score struck him as a portent of doom, every Cork one as a brave but probably futile act of resistance. It was like watching a match alongside Cassandra the Trojan prophetess of doom. He shook his head, wiped the sweat from his brow, winced, grimaced and sought reassurance that didn't reassure him at all.

The teams were level again just coming up to half-time when Alan Connolly got the ball thirty yards out on the right wing. I'd wager no one in Semple Stadium thought, *Here's a goal chance*. No one except Connolly, who swept in from the wing at speed past two defenders and, as a third closed in, shot past Barry Hogan. It was a breath-taking illustration of how great goal scorers have an internal computer that calculates the odds differently from everyone else. They're always thinking goal.

Goalscorers of this kind are a special breed. There were great players, D.J. Carey, Séamus Callanan, Joe Canning, who scored a lot of goals but whose goals were merely a function of their overall greatness. Their championship scoring tallies, 36–165 for Carey, 40–226 for Callanan, 27–486 for Canning, showed that. The specialist goalscorer's ratio is very different: 30–33 for the emblematic Seánie O'Leary; 40–56, 18–38 and 16–34 for the great wrecking-ball full-forwards Tony Doran, Joe McKenna and Christy Heffernan; 14–8 in the brief explosive career of Cork's John Fitzgibbon. It was a question of not just intention but instinct, the latter typified by O'Leary's goal for Cork in the 1984 All-Ireland final against Offaly. Jimmy Barry-Murphy's pass to O'Leary is behind him and keeper Damien Martin is almost on top of him but he takes one touch to make space and with the second sweeps the ball home while falling backwards. Like all the great opportunists, he makes the finish look simple and inevitable when it was neither.

Every county had their three-point aficionado – Eddie Brennan (26–63) for Kilkenny, Lar Corbett (29–80) for Tipperary, Waterford's Dan Shanahan (21–58) – but Cork traditionally abounded in them. As well as O'Leary and Fitzgibbon, you had Jimmy Barry-Murphy (23–52), Ray Cummins (18–46) and Kevin Hennessy (23–49), who found the net in the 1986 and 1990 final victories against Galway when Cork, scoring nine to their opponents' four, showed the power of goals to turn games.

Connolly was in this tradition. Successive hat-tricks in the league against Offaly and Wexford had whetted the appetite and now he was doing the same in the championship.

Goal two arrived early in the second half, the Blackrock man robbing a defender and sauntering down the middle to score. 'The new Ray Cummins, the new Ray Cummins,' exulted my neighbour before, for the second time, beating a tattoo on the back of the man and bear-hugging the woman just in front of him. It was just a momentary respite from worry. 'Too easy, too early,' he muttered and started to worry about the size of Cork's lead. 'Six isn't enough, we need to be seven up'; 'We need to get to eight'; 'Come on, we have to be ten ahead to be safe.'

Even Connolly's third goal, again from a position where another forward might have settled for a point, didn't entirely relax him. 'Good man, Downey, that's brilliant' was followed instantly by 'For fuck's sake, Downey, that's terrible.'

'There's supporters for you,' said a Youghal man the other side of me who was knocking great enjoyment out of the antics.

Not till the final quarter did my right-hand man admit victory. The match had become a rout and the winning margin would be a record for Cork against Tipp. At last he could bask in the glory of it all. 'Tipp are terrible. They have players who wouldn't get on a junior team in Cork.'

'This'll be remembered.'

We all looked over to locate the source of this interjection.

'This'll be remembered for a long time.'

He was a man in his early forties, staring at the voluble Cork enthusiast and in that state where someone's words are propelled through their lips by sheer force of temper as their head shakes with the effort to contain it.

'Whatever happened between Tipperary and Cork, we always respected Cork even when we beat them. We know what we're like, there's no need telling us.'

The young girl in the Tipperary jersey with him looked mortified but he kept going in this vein. He was being unfair, Tipp danced on the graves of defeated opponents with no less vigour than anyone else, but to see his county lay down their weapons like this must have been a shock to the system. Two years ago they'd been the whipping boys of the round robin but manager Colm Bonnar had been summarily scapegoated and sacked. Liam Cahill, who'd worked wonders with Waterford, was welcomed home as a messiah. The year before, Tipp beat Clare, drew with Limerick and Cork and looked like a team on the way up. Now they were back to square zero.

My neighbour didn't say a word after that. In fact there were still three minutes left when, with a sad and somewhat defeated air, he said to the guy next to him, 'Come on, we'll go,' and apologised to the couple in front of him: 'I get a bit carried away sometimes.' That he hadn't even known the couple he'd spent so much time pummelling and embracing came as something of a surprise. Maybe the Tipp man considered his comments a small victory for the Premier County or maybe he was embarrassed when he thought about them later. Either way he was distinctly lacking in the Hozier spirit.

The Cork fans poured on to the pitch as they'd done after the Limerick game. There was a giddy feeling about the way the team's fortunes had turned completely around in the space of just nine days. It seemed like anything could happen from here on in.

As I inched out of the stands, a wiry lad my own age edged over to me with the furtive air of a man seeking to sell some weed. He looked quickly all round him before saying in a low voice, 'I'm from Limerick.'

There was a conspiratorial tone to his voice, my lack of county colours perhaps having recommended me as someone with no partisan interest in today's game. 'Limerick should play for a draw against Waterford because if it's a draw Cork will be knocked out. I'm worried about Cork, they're the only team that can stop Limerick.'

Then he was gone, like a traveller in a time machine who'd come briefly back to warn me about the future.

As we walked back into Liberty Square, its great welcoming expanse lying before us as though expressly designed for days like this, a horse box was paused in traffic. Its occupant cast a cold equine eye on human life and passed by.

12

Sliding Doors

IT WASN'T TILL THE MONDAY MORNING AFTER the Limerick–Waterford match in the Gaelic Grounds that I became confident of finishing my championship journey.

There'd been a couple of earlier tests, the long delay on the platform in Killarney and the clamorous anarchy of the train to Thurles, but I came through them without too much difficulty. That Monday morning in Limerick was the big one. For a moment it felt like things could go either way. This was my *Sliding Doors* moment in Colbert Station.

I was rushing to catch the train out of Limerick after being held up by the discovery of a terrific little bookshop that announced itself with the sign *We don't do bestsellers but come in and you might find something you like.* The sign was right.

'My brother picks them and I sell them,' said the extremely nice middle-aged woman behind the till as I doubled the weight of my luggage.

The race against the clock, the weight of the bag and the size of the train I'd be taking to Limerick Junction combined to unsettle my painstakingly maintained equilibrium. The memory of the terrible panic attack on the Galway train the previous year flooded uncontrollably back. The station was different but it was the same kind of train.

The old familiar apprehension began to build. I found myself hoping the train wouldn't be packed again. But it was. There was one spare seat opposite a woman and a child clad in Clare hurling garb. The resemblance to the train the previous year was undeniable. It felt like an attempt to recreate the journey conditions as an experiment. I thought to myself that if things were going to go haywire again this was where and when it'd happen. We heard the announcement about this being the train to Limerick Junction. The hiss told me the doors were locked and that there was no way out now.

But as the train began to pull away like a hungover athlete lumbering out of his blocks I felt no more trepidation than if I'd been going to the kitchen to make a cup of tea. It was over. The tide had gone out on the days of fear and trembling. I felt like dancing down the carriage and bursting into Hollywood-musical-style song.

Before that morning, every trip had been accompanied by

a lump in the throat and a pain in the chest. I felt like a man carrying a valuable vase across a slippery floor. One misstep and it would slide out of my hands and shatter. After that morning the journey became something to enjoy rather than endure. It was pure gravy from then on in.

How had this change happened? The honest truth is that I didn't exactly know. My best guess is a combination of medication, desperation, compensation and determination. The tablets steadied the ship sufficiently for me to tackle the problem. I also felt that this was now or never. Like a team looking for an injury-time goal to stave off defeat, I was driven on by a sense of urgency. The prospect of losing out on the money the publishers had advanced for the book increased my resolve. I was in no position to be turning down money. But even all these factors couldn't entirely prevent me from feeling shaky in those opening championship weeks. I had to battle through the fear. Somehow, by a mysterious means I was almost afraid to analyse, the centre was holding. After over twenty years of shrinking, my horizons were suddenly expanding. And it felt OK. Sometimes, dare I say it, it actually felt good. I'd hit town the previous day to watch Limerick play Waterford in the final round-robin match for both teams. My furtive friend from Semple Stadium hadn't been the only one enamoured with the idea that Limerick might engineer a draw with Waterford to eliminate Cork. The more conspiratorially inclined Rebel fans also speculated on the possibility in the run-up to the game. The idea was a non-runner because a defeat for Limerick would put the champions out, which left an impossibly thin line between Machiavellian master stroke and suicidal miscalculation. Hurling was just too fast, too fluid and too unpredictable to attempt a cover version of the 1982 West Germany–Austria World Cup match. Limerick would be much keener to recover the blow to their pride inflicted by their utterly unexpected loss to Cork.

The electioneering continued on the afternoon of the match. Outside the Gaelic Grounds Billy Kelleher, whose perma-tanned handsomeness made him look like an adulterous oilman in an eighties soap opera, was being introduced to the voters by Willie O'Dea, who as always looked like he'd put on a false nose and moustache disguise to rob a bank and forgot to remove it. Willie had the proprietorial air of someone showing off his ranch. You could practically hear the keys to the city jingling in his pocket. Limerick was his lady. A few yards further on Labour's Niamh Hourigan cut a much more diffident figure but was flanked by two beautiful dogs. Seán Kelly was represented in hologram form on a large screen, like the Red Skull in *Captain America: The Winter Soldier*.

I was on another terrace behind another goal but the vibe was different from the evening in Cork. Rain began to fall as 'Thunderstruck' by AC/DC boomed from the stadium's PA.

Limerick's sound system seemed louder and more bass-heavy than those at other provincial grounds. It made you feel like you were at a gig. When the opening notes of a song I'd never heard before rang out a group of Limerick fans whooped with delight and began to sing and dance along with it as though it was a local anthem. Jesus, I thought, this is a brilliant song. My daughters would later inform me that almost everyone else had heard 'What Do You Want to Know' by Michael Maloney yonks ago. He'd sung it at Limerick's homecoming after the previous year's All-Ireland. 'It's one of our songs in the dressing room and when it goes off we go off with it,' John Kiely had said.

Maloney was actually from Ardara in Donegal but I could see why the song struck a chord with Limerick. There was a winning insolence to this tale of someone's head being wrecked by small-town gossip. At the heart of its brilliance was a certain what-the-fuck-are-you-looking-at quality.

Limerick were warming up in front of us as it played and driving balls over the top of the net behind the goals out of pre-match exuberance. The same thing had happened in Páirc Uí Chaoimh where some marvellous catches testified to the magnificent hand and eye co-ordination of the hurling community. The problem in Limerick was that the overcast nature of the afternoon made it really difficult to pick up the flight of the sliotar so the effect was of being subjected to a barrage. 'Look at your man,' someone said, 'he's after getting his nose broken by the ball.' I looked and saw a middle-aged man holding a bloody handkerchief to his nose as the fusillade continued.

Thoughts of an upset disappeared when I looked down the other end of the pitch. The terrace was half-empty, the Waterford turn-out poor. This was odd on the face of it: the Déise had beaten Cork, drawn with Tipperary and lost by a point to Clare in a much better than expected campaign. But you can gauge a lot about a team by their supporters' attitude towards it. Most Waterford fans didn't think their side had a hope.

Within about five minutes you could see that Waterford agreed with them. Limerick were not a dirty team, accusations in that vein largely proceeded from jealousy, but they were an intimidating one. They were big, they were combative, they were mentally very focused and physically very strong. It wasn't just the giants like Hayes and Hegarty and Diarmaid Byrnes. There was a photo taken after their win over Clare in the classic 2022 Munster final which showed the full-back line of Mike Casey, Dan Morrissey and Seán Finn in the dressing room wearing nothing but their shorts. The impressive abdominal musculature on show made the shot look like a cross between a *Magic Mike* poster and an ad for whey protein. Wrestling these guys off the ball would be a tall order.

From the start Limerick's physical edge over Waterford was so pronounced the visitors looked like precocious minors trying to find their bearings at senior level. Every 50:50 contest, every physical tussle went Limerick's way. The half-back line, leaky as a colander against Cork, was so dominant it was like a forcefield. Donald Trump would have loved to build a wall this impenetrable.

The first quarter of the match was entirely one-sided but this wasn't reflected in the scoreline because Limerick put together the greatest exhibition of bad shooting I'd seen in my life. They'd win the ball, cut through Waterford, make space for the shot and then it would tail wide. The crowd behind the goal were utterly bemused. They'd get ready to acclaim a point and next thing it would fly just the wrong side of the post. Most of the shots didn't miss by much but by the tenth minute Limerick had hit nine wides.

Normally you'd predict that a team would regret this profligacy later on but it still didn't seem there was any way Limerick could lose. The serial inaccuracy was just an intriguing sideshow en route to the inevitable. But when Shane Bennett flicked his brother Stephen's free past Nickie Quaid midway through the half, Waterford were three points up after being completely outplayed.

It was a bit like the moment in *The Mark of Zorro* when Tyrone Power, whose great-grandfather came from Waterford, says after Basil Rathbone nicks him on the arm during the greatest sword fight in movie history, 'I needed that scratch to awaken me.' Roused from their slumber Limerick hit ten points before half-time to lead by five, with Tom Morrissey, the swashbuckling Power figure of their attack, and Hayes, their intriguingly villainous Rathbone, to the fore.

Another Bennett goal left just two points in it entering the final quarter. A shock or even the tactical draw was still theoretically on the cards but you could sense Limerick bending the game to their will with every passing minute. By the end they had ten points to spare, their final quarter having been so tyrannically inexorable I left the Gaelic Grounds convinced the Cork result was just an odd freak of nature. Nobody was going to stop this juggernaut.

Waterford were out and few teams had ever been so unlucky to make an early exit. They'd effectively have qualified for the next stage with two games to spare had they held on to a four-point injury-time lead over Tipperary in their second match. Tipp got a goal and a point to scrape a draw. The injury-time heartbreak against Clare followed and in Limerick they played like a team that knew its chance was already gone.

Their manager would be gone soon afterwards. Waterford's championship performance had been pretty good but the county seemed to have made up its mind about Davy Fitzgerald after a disastrous league campaign. All the psychodrama which surrounded him made it easy to forget that Fitzgerald was a very good manager. He'd won an All-Ireland with an unfancied Clare team, brought Waterford to a first final in forty-five years, won a first Leinster title in fifteen years and almost reached a first All-Ireland final in twenty-three with a Wexford team that was going nowhere before he arrived. Fitzgerald was hurling's great salvage expert. He'd improved all those teams and none of them got better when he left them. Yet the relationships seemed to go sour. You could see why. His hyperactive blend of combativeness and complaint was tiring enough to watch on TV, God knows what it was like to deal with on a regular basis.

Perhaps a feeling that Davy was 'too much' deprived him of jobs he seemed eminently qualified for. Dublin and Galway both changed managers that summer and looked elsewhere. Fitzgerald was rumoured to have coveted these jobs but ended up taking charge of Antrim. It seemed a significant downgrade but it was likely he'd improve that team too. How long would this relationship last? I imagined him in thirty years still going from county to county and being announced as the new Fermanagh boss. Once I'd joined in the general chorus of disapproval aimed at his antics on the side line. Now those antics seemed to me as being not so much aimed at their ostensible targets as being the way a highly strung man got through the stress of the job. It might have been better to understand more and condemn less. We all have our ways of getting through.

The round robin was over. Clare would play Limerick in the Munster final for a third year running. Cork would have to make their way through the qualifier system. It'd be fascinating to see how it all panned out.

13

Castlehaven Nights

AFTER ALL THAT HURLING, IT'S TIME TO RETURN to the football championship. Don't worry, you haven't missed anything. That was the problem.

From the start of April to the middle of May, football had lumbered through provincial championships with very little bearing on a competition where the top sixteen qualifiers had already been effectively decided. Now at last it was time for some meaningful games.

Only joking. The sixteen remaining teams would now spend a month in four groups playing twenty-four games to reduce their number by just four. A strategy expressly designed to suck the life out of the competition couldn't have done any better. They might at least have opted for the more logical eight qualifiers. Instead the top three out of four got through and before a ball was kicked everyone knew who the bottom side in each group would be.

There was some pretence that winning the group would be vital because, just as no one expects the Spanish Inquisition, *no one wants to be in the preliminary quarter-final.* But Galway would end up at this dreaded destination and go all the way to the final. After much thought and tinkering the GAA had ended up with one of the worst competition structures in the history of mankind. No one liked it, interest was waning and crowds were down.

Cork's decision to play Donegal not in Páirc Uí Chaoimh but in Páirc Uí Rinn, the county's boutique secondary inter-county venue, was an acknowledgement that the football championship's appeal had become more selective.

The one interesting thing in the provincials was Donegal's annexation of the Ulster title. It was a 'return of the king' moment.

Perhaps no one had ever received more praise for managing a team to All-Ireland success than Jim McGuinness had when Donegal won the 2012 title. The plaudits were deserved – he'd effectively brought them from nowhere in two years. But other managers, Seán Boylan with Meath in 1996 and John O'Mahony with Galway in 1998, had done the same without the same mystique attaching to their achievement. The difference was that something about McGuinness invited the perception of him as a guru figure.

He'd entitled his autobiography *Until Victory Always*, referencing a famous quote ('Hasta la victoria siempre') from a letter Che Guevara wrote to Fidel Castro. You actually could imagine McGuinness, driven, implacably serious, haunted, wearing camouflage fatigues in a jungle clearing and delivering his latest communiqué on the iniquities of imperialism. Or perhaps as a Marxist academic parsing the implications of that communiqué because there was something scholarly about McGuinness. Wheels seemed to be constantly whirring behind that poker-faced façade. His seriousness was not an affectation. The driven quality perhaps stemmed in part from the tragic deaths of two brothers, one from a heart attack at the age of sixteen, another in a car crash in his twenties. McGuinness had been present on both occasions. How could anyone who hadn't suffered such losses imagine what he'd gone through?

Part of the fascination with McGuinness was that his ingenuity could shade into extremism. Donegal's semi-final loss to Dublin was sometimes held up as his archetypal coaching achievement. On the face of it, this made no sense considering they'd won the Sam Maguire the following year. But there was something awe-inspiring about Donegal's 2011 performance against the Dubs. It was the *ne plus ultra* of negative football. No one had ever seen anything like it. In its determination to take things to the absolute limit, it resembled one of the interminable shrieking saxophone solos of late-period John Coltrane.

Donegal had actually played lots of attractive football in their All-Ireland-winning year but the abiding impression of the 2011 semi-final stereotyped McGuinness as the nabob of negativity who'd set football on the course hitting a dead end so resoundingly in the summer of 2024.

The aura surrounding him was such that many people believed McGuinness would actually succeed in his ambition of becoming a successful soccer manager though he had no background in the sport. It hadn't worked out. There'd been a spell on the backroom staff at Celtic and with a club in Beijing but when managerial opportunity knocked in 2019, with Charlotte Independence of the USL Championship, he was sacked after just one win in fourteen games.

When Declan Bonner quit the Donegal job in 2022 there was a brief flurry of speculation that McGuinness might be tempted to return and link up one last time with Michael Murphy, the county's greatest ever footballer and a key figure in the revolutionary war of 2011–14. Instead Donegal plumped for Paddy Carr, a veteran whose only inter-county experience dated back two decades. By the end of a catastrophic season they'd won three games out of twelve and been relegated from division one, Carr had been sacked and Murphy had retired. They were at their lowest ebb in over a decade. This was the moment McGuinness chose to take the job. He likes a challenge.

McGuinness' return was accompanied by huge excitement

but limited expectation. Donegal had fallen well off the pace. He was a great manager but he wasn't a miracle-worker. The players weren't there this time. It'd take longer than two years to get this team challenging for honours.

Donegal won six of their seven games in division two, drew the other and beat Armagh in the league final. A few eyebrows were raised but it was division two after all. Reality would intrude when they met Derry in the first round of the Ulster championship. Derry also had a new manager of illustrious pedigree, Mickey Harte, whose three All-Ireland victories with Tyrone was one of the modern game's great achievements. They'd enjoyed the same kind of league campaign as Donegal but in division one. Their victory over Dublin in a league final entertaining enough to engender fantasies about an imminent attacking renaissance made them many people's favourites for the All-Ireland.

Donegal travelled to Celtic Park and beat the home team by six points. Then they beat Tyrone in extra-time and Armagh after a penalty shoot-out to win the Ulster title. Now we were paying attention. The weekend before they arrived in Cork they'd overwhelmed Tyrone. After eleven undefeated games, this juggernaut was picking up speed all the time. Maybe McGuinness was a miracle-worker after all.

The number of Donegal fans who'd made the marathon trek south suggested they believed so. In the league Donegal had beaten Cork by eleven points. A similar result wasn't beyond the bounds of possibility. Seeking a seat in the stand I bumped into Christy Collins and Dan Buckley. 'We might be in for a tough afternoon,' said Christy. Dan concurred.

I'd travelled with Christy and Dan to my first match in Páirc Uí Chaoimh, the 1999 football league final between Dublin and Cork. I'd been living in Castletownshend for a few months at the time. Christy owned the busiest of the three local pubs and it was there I first became familiar with the legend of Castlehaven. He was one of seven brothers, Dinty, Francis, Donal, Bernard, Anthony and Vincent were the others, who'd played a key role in the club's amazing seventies rise from Junior B football to a senior county final.

Christy was one of those big rangy midfielders who'd abounded during an age when high fielding was a more central part of the game. They were often builders or farmers, the power in their frames of a kind you only get from hard physical work. He was good enough to make the Cork team and be handed one of the most difficult tasks in GAA history: marking Jack O'Shea when that greatest of midfielders was at his peak. 'I spent an afternoon chasing around Killarney after him,' he quipped to me once.

Dan was a quietly spoken farmer whose main contribution had been behind the scenes. When they'd reached the historic 1979 county final he'd been club chairman. Forty-five years later he was club president. Between them Christy and Dan had an awful lot of the qualities which keep GAA clubs going.

Dan's son Kevin was an example of the changing face of rural Ireland. In 2003 he and his colleague Matthew Lawlor set up a tech company in Skibbereen called Spearline. Twenty years later it was bought by the Silicon Valley firm Cyara. By that stage Spearline was employing over 200 people between Cork, Waterford and India. A lot of Castlehaven people were very proud of this but if you asked them what Spearline actually did the answer was usually 'something to do with phone lines'.

Considerable technical wizardry was obviously involved but my own illiteracy in these matters means I'm not much wiser after reading on Cyara's website that Spearline 'brings expanded in-country dialing capabilities as well as assurance for voice and video-based communications across WebRTC, VoIP, fixed-line and cellular networks'. Something with phone lines, in other words. The magnitude of the achievement doesn't stop my abiding memory of Kevin Buckley being of a man selling club lottery tickets door to door on wintry nights back in the day. Beat that, Mark Zuckerberg.

The Road to Croker ends with a chapter about Castlehaven winning the county final which includes an over-confident assertion that now I knew what the GAA meant to people. That was only true on a very superficial level. It was several years later before I really knew how a local club could be the most important thing in people's lives. That was because for a few years it was one of the most important things in mine.

The process by which I became utterly enraptured by Castlehaven began with a moment not of triumph but of defeat. Favourites to win the 2011 county final, they lost by five points to UCC. The defeat looked different when four of the college team, Peter Crowley, Johnny Buckley, Paul Geaney and Stephen O'Brien, won All-Ireland medals with Kerry just three years later, but at the time it was gutting. Back home after the game I wondered whether to go to Union Hall that night. I'd go. The place would be like a morgue but I'd go.

On landing in the village it was very hard to distinguish this night from the triumphant one eight years previously. The pubs were packed, the fans were out and so were the players. The only tell-tale difference was that the match was hardly mentioned. An occasional sotto voce discussion was the sole proof it had ever happened. It was as though a communal decision had been taken to buoy up the team's spirit with this show of solidarity. They say that victory has a hundred fathers and defeat is an orphan. That night defeat had two hundred fathers. And mothers too.

It was all too much for one of the players, who burst out, 'I can't take this. Everyone is being so nice to us and we let you all down. We lost.' The supporters just smiled and said nothing. They were playing a long game because they knew this was the very best way to get the players to put in a big effort next season. They did, and the following year we were back to celebrate a triumph by one point over Duhallow. This time everyone talked about the match, every last kick of it. The players danced and displayed the trophy from a platform in the centre of the village and the pubs stayed open till six in the morning.

Nights like this with their feelings of communal togetherness and unbridled celebration had an 'all bets are off' feeling as though you'd entered an arena where the usual rules didn't apply. People looked out for each other. After one of the finals I remember a player's mother trawling the village in the early hours for waifs and strays before touring the countryside to drop us all home.

I got to know people I'd known for years better than I'd ever known them before and I got to know the club at a deeper level. I watched one former player deliver a recitation about the glories of Castlehaven. Tears were streaming down his face and down the faces of some listeners too. When the club asked me to be the guest speaker at that year's dinner dance I felt genuinely honoured and worried for weeks about whether I'd be up to the task.

A second successive title came against Nemo Rangers, the historic kings of Cork club football with a reputation for near invincibility in county finals (they'd played twenty-one and won eighteen of them). Brian Hurley kicked twelve points, Haven won by two and it seemed like the apotheosis of the club's achievement. The unlikely journey from rural anonymity had become a never-ending story. Afterwards we were drinking in

Larry Tompkins' pub on the city quays when a club official asked me if I wanted to travel down on the team bus.

I liked them an awful lot, the players, their mentors, their parents, their wives and girlfriends, their supporters, the whole experience of these decent good-humoured hard-working people striving together to make something memorable and enjoying when it happened. It was a fantastic thing to witness and the great thing was that dozens of villages and towns all over the country got to experience this every summer. The GAA is an unrivalled machine for the production of communal joy. And of excitement.

Rural life has many good qualities but excitement is not one of them. It's one reason youngsters leave, perhaps coming back later in life when more prosaic considerations increase in importance. County final victories provide a welcome injection of the unexpected, the memorable and the spectacular. They shorten the winters. They're the closest thing Ireland gets to those frenetic cavalcades, horns honking, people hanging out of windows and dancing on car roofs in heaving city plazas which greet Latin American soccer victories. The types of villages passing motorists dismiss with a quip about sleepiness are suddenly possessed by the carnival spirit.

On the way home from the county final win over Nemo the team bus drew to a halt a few miles outside Union Hall. By the side of the road were tables laden with the products of West Cork Distillers, another local success story. I've never felt more honoured in my life than I did when lowering brandy by the side of a ditch along with the Haven panel in a rural darkness illuminated only by bus headlights. The glamorous life at last. That night I slept in the same house as the Andy Scannell Cup.

A decade later Castlehaven occupied much less space on my emotional radar. Back in 2014, they still mattered a great deal to me when their loss of a county final replay to Nemo might have been the most disappointing result of my life. It took a toll on the team. Haven entered a period of transition and so did I.

I still got to their matches but the consuming passion of old wasn't there. This was partly because I'd started writing a Monday column for the *Irish Independent* and the necessity to watch everything happening on Sunday precluded going to club games. My mental state didn't help either. There were days I could have gone but just couldn't face the journey. Haven's victory in the county final over Nemo in 2023 came as I was taking my first tentative steps towards addressing my travel phobia.

The fire might also have died down because even at the height of my obsession I knew Castlehaven wasn't really my club. I'd chosen it whereas most of the people I knew had inherited it. I'd essentially been looking in from the outside. But the nature of the welcome I received meant I never felt like a tourist. I felt like a guest.

I'll always be grateful for that. Someone said to me at the time that my view of the players and the club was too romantic. Maybe they were right. Yet those Haven days and nights gave me a chance to feel really rooted in a community for the first time in my life, to feel that sense of belonging which is at the heart of the GAA.

Lately I've become more sceptical about the old ideas of community and belonging and more aware of the ways they can exclude as well as include. I still think the GAA represents the most positive form of those concepts. Its notion of community is a fundamentally benign and inclusive one. You don't see GAA clubs lending their support to anti-immigrant protests. You did see the association inviting the Irish Muslim community to celebrate the Eid al-Adha festival when mosques were closed by Covid restrictions.

One of my daughters is an avid Castlehaven fan who travelled to the 2022 county final on the supporters' bus. 'I love it,' she says, 'because it's not even really sport. It's a community thing, like the threshing at Tragumna.'

On the biggest championship days, the GAA can look like just one more sporting organisation, an Irish version of the Premier League or the NFL. The threshing match aspect still underpins it all. It's what makes the GAA unique and anyone failing to take that into account gets only half the picture. I learned that in Castlehaven. Christy Collins and Dan Buckley were two of my teachers and as we chatted in Páirc Uí Rinn that afternoon I wanted Cork to win for their sake. That was how I'd felt about Castlehaven. I looked at the people around me and thought how great a win would be for them. For them. Not for me. Not in the same way. I was interested but they were implicated.

The gulf in status between the Cork hurling and football teams was obvious in the difference between the mild atmosphere in Páirc Uí Rinn and the feverish one at Semple Stadium a fortnight earlier.

When the hurlers were going well they commandeered almost all the county's emotional bandwidth. Yet only three counties had won more football All-Irelands than Cork and there were large swathes of the county where not only was football the number one game but hurling was no stronger than in the likes of Derry, Kildare or Tyrone. Nevertheless the football devotees were treated like members of a minority religion, tolerated, sometimes encouraged but always the subject of condescension from those hewing to the one true faith.

Donegal were brimming with confidence that afternoon. They monopolised possession early on and engaged in the prolonged passing moves which had become football's bane. Except theirs were different. They'd seem to be petering out in pedestrian fashion when someone, usually a defender, would produce a burst of pace which unhinged the defence sufficiently to create an opportunity. It might be Ryan McHugh, Ciarán Moore, Eoghan Bán Gallagher or, most strikingly, Peadar Mogan.

Mogan had been a good defender previously but McGuinness had converted him into an unstoppable and blisteringly fast secret weapon. When he won Player of the Month awards in May and June, it looked like this might be 'Peadar Mogan summer'.

The visitors led by two points at the end of the first quarter but looked completely in control. Then Cork turned them over in midfield and Mattie Taylor, like Jordan Hayes in Portlaoise, found himself clear with half the field ahead and only the keeper to beat. The keeper in question, Shaun Patton, who'd been out the field, sprinted back towards the Donegal goal for fear of being lobbed. He made it but a few seconds later Taylor arrived and stuck the ball past him. It seemed we'd have a game after all, but when Donegal scored six of the half's last seven points the identity of its winners still seemed obvious.

A couple of minutes into the second half Cork cut through the middle and Seán Powter sent a rocket past Patton. Thirty seconds later Brian Hurley chased back, dispossessed an opponent and set in motion a chain of events which saw a shot for a point blocked down, a couple of players bat the ball around in the air, Chris Óg Jones scuff a first-time shot, Patton parry it into the air and Rory Maguire arrive up from the half-back line to fist the loose ball into the net. It was the type of glorious chaos which can upset the workings of the most precise system. Cork were suddenly four points up and the conclusion looked a lot less foregone.

It was as though someone had put a few hundred non-lethal volts through the Cork supporters. The crowd of 7,451 felt huge because deciding to play in Páirc Uí Rinn was a masterstroke. Spectators who'd have been lost in the wide-open spaces of Páirc Uí Chaoimh filled the much smaller ground. There was an intensity about their support you wouldn't have got in the bigger stadium where getting super fervent would seem slightly embarrassing with banks of empty seats looming in front of you. It was the difference between watching a band in the 3Arena and watching them in the Olympia.

The crowd responded to the Cork players, the players responded to Cork, and Donegal got stuck in too. The rest of the match consisted of the favourites trying to run down the outsiders with the inexorable dedication of the trackers pursuing Butch Cassidy and the Sundance Kid to the edge of a cliff.

Cork were not the greatest team but they chased, tackled and never shirked a challenge. These artisan qualities are prized above all others in Gaelic football. There's a special approving flavour to the cheer afforded a player who hurtles towards the ball even though it's obvious he's going to ship punishment by doing so. A player who shirks a challenge, lets his head drop or gives up running is in breach of his contract with the crowd. Cork had taken a couple of terrible beatings from Kerry when it looked like they'd run up the white flag. It damaged the morale of fans as much as that of the players.

Cleary had turned the team into one which played with the tight-knit attitude of an overachieving club side. It played like Castlehaven.

Donegal kept coming and levelled just before the start of injury-time. All Cork's efforts would be in vain if they lost by even a point. Anything but victory would be greeted by those who weren't there with a shrug and a 'same old story'. Just as things seemed to have turned Donegal's way, Cork sub Steven Sherlock struck a great point. The Rebels had something to hold on to in the last few minutes.

The siege in those minutes was so unrelenting I found myself thinking as I did when England put the Irish goal under non-stop pressure in 1988: 'Just score, will you, and put us out of our misery.' But Donegal didn't score. A gap would open up and a couple of desperate defenders would converge to close it. McHugh had a chance to level it but dropped his shot short and, with time almost up, Cork had the last word.

Full-back Daniel O'Mahony went for it and burst over the half-way line like a man breaking out of prison. The home fans saw that, with Donegal having thrown everyone forward, Cork had men over. There was a great release of tension and as O'Mahony surged on the noise grew. He played a one-two with Ian Maguire and kept going. The crowd roared as though cheering a parade. It was as though this run was a gesture of defiance against everyone who'd mocked this much-maligned team. O'Mahony slipped the ball to midfielder Colm

O'Callaghan, who fisted it over the bar. This time it really was the wise option.

Less than a minute later Cork fans were invading the pitch and a Donegal woman next to me asked, 'Does that mean we're out?' I opted against treating her to my staple diatribe against the structure of the championship and just said, 'No, no, ye're grand. Ye'll get through to the next round no problem.' I walked across the pitch. The numbers were smaller but the jubilation had a hurling-sized intensity. As I was going out the gate an old guy said to me, 'Fair play to Cleary, he should have had that job ten years ago.' This was so in tune with my own thinking you may wonder if he's an apocryphal figure. Not at all.

Everything in this book really happened. What's the point otherwise? I wouldn't have the imagination to invent all of it.

Cork football hadn't had a day like this in years. An honest team and an honest manager deserved it. They lost their next game against Tyrone after a sending-off at a crucial moment and were eliminated by Louth after the nervousness missing against Donegal returned as they lost by a point. It had still been a good season for them on balance and the county board offered Cleary another year as manager. That afternoon against Donegal was a glimpse of what they could be at their best.

The defeat didn't seem to affect Donegal in the least. Two weeks later they beat Clare by twenty-four points and ended up going two rounds further in the competition than Cork.

Did this justify my criticism of the qualifiers for containing too many meaningless games? Perhaps. Yet Cork–Donegal was one of only two really good football games I saw that summer and the other also turned out to mean nothing in retrospect.

Maybe that didn't matter because they were great while they were going on. After all, we don't watch live games in retrospect.

14

The Bad, the Good and the Dubs

KILLARNEY, THURLES, LIMERICK AND THE TWO Cork grounds had all been great but I'd finally found a stadium I didn't like. Bereft of atmosphere, impersonal and half-empty, it seemed the worst possible place to watch a game. Yep, Croke Park really sucked.

I'm being unfair. Fantastic days lay ahead at the daddy of all Irish sporting venues. But a crowd of less than 50,000 doesn't show headquarters off to best effect. An 82,000-capacity stadium can make a crowd which would fill any other GAA ground seem small. The empty spaces rival the spectators in dictating the overall effect. There were just 35,484 at the Leinster hurling final between Kilkenny and Dublin.

Croke Park can also make a bad game seem worse. The absence of the buzzing crowd noise which attends a properly exciting match makes the huge spaces of the stand feel lonely and unforgiving. There's no worse place to watch your team take a beating.

A perfect storm was blowing that Saturday evening. The crowd wasn't big enough for the stadium and the game was one of the worst sporting contests I'd ever seen. It was certainly one of the most one-sided. Even the Kilkenny fans seemed bored by it.

I should have gone to the following day's Munster final between Limerick and Clare instead but I couldn't get a ticket. Maybe I'd have gone to the Leinster final anyway in memory of my father who'd always taken the boldly contrarian position that the Munster decider was much over-rated by comparison with its rival to the east.

It had seemed a promising fixture. The Dublin hurling revival, like the jazz revival or the Irish-language revival, is something that's always about to happen and never does. This year's portents were particularly promising. The Galway–Kilkenny match a few weeks previously had been regarded as a shadow-boxing workout before they renewed rivalries in a third successive final. A fortnight previously Dublin put the kibosh on that by beating Galway in Pearse Stadium, eliminating the home team and signalling an end to Henry Shefflin's western managerial adventure.

The worry so evidently consuming Shefflin on the Salthill sideline proved prophetic. After that draw, Galway had been well beaten by Wexford before Dublin finished them off. They'd been unlucky that a questionable sending-off for David Burke changed the shape of the game but it had been a struggle all summer. There'd been an odd, inchoate feeling about Shefflin's three years in charge. Galway reminded me of a comedy sketch I'd once seen about a bunch of guys who try to build a house by montage and end up with an unconnected bunch of blocks. Shefflin's Galway had been a montage team. They could be brilliant in flashes but you kept waiting for them to put it all together consistently in even just one game.

Shefflin had perhaps gambled on glory in Galway, leaving him in pole position to succeed Brian Cody when the greatest manager in hurling history finally stepped down. Cody's frosty attitude when their teams met suggested he regarded his former star's pivot to opposition as verging on the treasonous. When Cody did step down Derek Lyng got the job, beat Shefflin in Leinster and got to the All-Ireland final. Lyng, a workman to Shefflin's emperor during their playing days, was the slow and steady tortoise who'd won the race.

Shefflin would eventually be replaced by Mícheál Donoghue, the manager who'd cooked the former Top Cat's goose by masterminding Dublin's win in Galway. Donoghue's presence was a big reason to suspect Dublin would give a good account of themselves against Kilkenny. A notably shrewd operator, he'd brought Galway a first All-Ireland in twenty-nine years in 2017 before surprisingly stepping down two years later.

You expected Donoghue to have something up his sleeve for the Cats. Instead he togged out in a tactical T-shirt. Dublin started badly and got worse at a rate of knots which suggested a keenness to prove the concept of rock bottom didn't apply to hurling.

The match lasted about twelve minutes as a contest. Kilkenny were seven points up by then and Dublin clearly weren't going to come back. In fact it was probably over once Eoin Cody scored Kilkenny's first goal in the fourth minute. Four Dublin defenders had ambled towards a loose ball on the left wing before Cody, sensing his opportunity like a pickpocket who spots a wallet protruding from a pocket, snaffled it from under their noses, cut in and buried a shot past keeper Seán Brennan.

The pattern of the game became very simple. Dublin would puck the ball aimlessly down the field, unerringly picking out a Kilkenny player standing on his own. He'd then deliver a pass to a team-mate who, under very little pressure, would strike a long-range point. It was difficult to work out what Dublin actually intended to do.

Right in front of me sat a Dublin fan with his wife, son and daughter. As things went from worse to even worse again his only response was to utter variations on the word 'Jesus' like an actor executing an improvisatory voice exercise. *Jesus. Jaysus. Jeeeeeesus. Jesus Christ. Ah Jaysus.* The last despairing exclamation was prompted when Kilkenny scored their second goal after Brennan had spilled a routine high catch into the path of T.J. Reid, who flicked home.

The second half continued in the same predictable vein, Richie Reid picking off loose passes, Adrian Mullen, Cian Kenny and T.J. Reid shooting over the bar. My mind drifted to sentimental reveries about my late father. He'd be watching this down below, putting his hooves up with Charles Manson, Margaret Thatcher, Bon Scott and the inventor of call waiting while an avuncular Satan popped a few more coals on the fire, my father going on at such length about the innate superiority of 'da byze' from Kilkenny that his companions would think, *Yes, this is Hell alright.* I felt a warm glow at the thought of my father in a spot which held so many of his old friends, all those doughty gouty inter-county philanderers and Carroll's All-Star boozers who'd never have been happy with the insipid charms of the kingdom up above. You're dead right, he'd be saying to Bon Scott, whose old AC/DC colleagues would play Croke Park just two months later, hell ain't a bad place to be.

Limerick were powerful. Cork were explosive. Kilkenny were intelligent. Players found space and their team-mates found the free man. The mathematical precision with which they picked Dublin apart had been the Kilkenny way for years. The calm, systematic nature of their play made hurling look a very simple game. It took a lot of hard work to make things look this easy. No other county was as adept at sensing a weakness in the opposition and exploiting it. That had been easy enough today because Dublin's entire performance was one huge weakness. They were far from a bad team – only three weeks earlier they'd run Kilkenny to two points – but like an insect trying to free itself from a sundew plant, the harder they tried, the more hopeless their plight became.

Late in the second half Brennan tried to pick out a team-mate with a short puck-out. Unfortunately his cunning plan worked as well as one of Baldrick's in *Blackadder*. The team-mate was looking elsewhere and had no idea the ball had been played towards him. Mullen nipped in and passed to T.J. Reid, who scored Kilkenny's third goal. Today's pair might have been the easiest of his career. The man in front of me stared gloomily at the pitch and this time said nothing. This match had literally beaten the bejesus out of him. A visiting Spanish bullfighting aficionado might have wondered why people patronised such a cruel and one-sided spectacle.

My first Dublin trip for ages had been a black-and-amber washout. But there were far better days to come in the capital, days which would prove interesting in ways I didn't yet imagine.

The following Sunday I hit for Roscommon to see Mayo play Dublin in the last round of the football group-stage qualifiers. Waiting in Spiddal for the bus in to Galway I saw a man walking slowly and not altogether steadily through the village with the air of someone heading home on the morning after. The clothes were crumpled and creased like he'd slept in them or maybe thrown them on the floor beside a couch on which he'd passed out. 'Sure hang on, stay here for the night and we'll have a few more,' someone would have said. The most welcome idea in the world then, it seemed the worst one ever now. There's nothing lonelier than that morning road home with the beginnings of a hangover for company. It mightn't be there yet but it's in the post. He stopped next to me at the bus stop. I recognised that pained look in the eyes, as if the sun's rays were a personal affront. I'd seen it look back at me from more than enough mirrors.

'Where are you off to?'

I told him. He thought Roscommon was a long way to go for a match.

'Are you visiting around here?'

I told him the local connection and he seemed relieved, able to relax because he could place me. He told me about his time working in America and said I looked like my Uncle Ned, the greyhound man and plasterer. It wasn't the first time I'd heard this. There's a tell-tale stoop in the walk apparently. He told me his father was dead a couple of years and in that instant I got a picture of the Crúiscín Lán back in the seventies on one of those many nights when kids, placated with Pub Crisps and Coke, were having the eyes cut out of their heads with smoke, an Irish rite of passage largely gone the way of corporal punishment, thumbing lifts and shotgun weddings. Your man's father, a small wiry guy, was belting out a song, the pub falling quiet as the murderous tale unfolded. I named the song he used to sing.

'That was his song,' said your man and his eyes filled with tears. For a moment he seemed slightly overcome. I wasn't entirely steady either as we stood silently for a second and thought about the dead fathers of drinking sons. Then he smiled, wished me luck and pushed off for home. I hoped the memory might have done him some good and that he'd be alright. It was on a long morning's walk like this that I'd decided to knock the drink on the head for good.

Mayo and Dublin were already through but there would be something at stake because (trumpet fanfare) no one wanted to play in the preliminary quarter-finals. If the vehicle I caught outside Galway Cathedral wasn't exactly a mini-bus, it was certainly mini-bus adjacent. Sufficiently so to bring back memories of away trips with the school football team and the driver telling a lad who'd asked him for a cigarette, 'I don't supply monkeys with firearms.' We hit off to the sound of a DJ announcing her 'indie bangers', and Kings of Leon played us out of town. On we went. Through Moylough, birthplace of Galway footballing legend Enda Colleran. Through Ballygar, birthplace of Galway footballing legend Mattie McDonagh. Through Athleague, where killing time before a hurling match in the late eighties I'd stumbled on a bunch of lads watching a video of 9½ Weeks in a darkened pub.

The citizens of this hinterland were now being represented in Europe by new MEP Ciarán Mullooly whose conviction that he'd come with a late run proved correct.

My conviction that Mullooly had not actually gone over to the dark side of the force was borne out when he joined up with the centrist Renew Europe group in the European Parliament, triggering spectacular bursts of invective from the actual Irish far right who accused him of taking the seat under false pretences. The truth was that people had voted for Mullooly because they liked the 'rural first' politics he'd always stood for, not because they thought he was a Lanesboro Le Pen. I was pleased all the canvassing had borne fruit for him.

Roscommon town was teeming with Dubs. Advocates of Dublin playing more games outside Croke Park seemed to think this would greatly inconvenience the metropolitan horde. It was grand and easy for them to make Croke Park but would their delicate constitutions bear the rigours of a trek to Tullamore or even Longford? They'd be lost once they left the county boundaries. In fact the Dublin GAA fan loved to travel. The county had always been one of the few which brought decent crowds to away league games. A look at the centre of any popular Irish town on a summer Saturday night also serves to dispel the notion of the travel-shy jackeen. Keeping the hoors at home is the problem.

They certainly weren't outnumbered by the Mayo fans, who had a much shorter distance to travel. While that day's attendance of 16,870 was the largest of the qualifiers, it also showed their lack of pulling power. I'd bought a ticket as soon as they became available in the conviction the match would be a sell-out. How could it not be? Just a year earlier the two teams had been half of a quarter-final double bill which filled Croke Park to capacity. Cork and Derry were also in action but Dublin and Mayo easily accounted for the majority of fans. They were football's biggest draw. In 2019 their semi-final also filled Croke Park while the semi between Kerry and Tyrone attracted just 33,848 fans.

Surely they were guaranteed to sell out Hyde Park in a flash? Apparently not. The stadium would only be three-quarters full. The fans could have been accommodated in Markievicz Park, something which would have been dismissed as insane had anyone suggested it. There was a striking similarity between the Hyde Park attendance and the 14,789 figure from the counties' February national league meeting in Castlebar. That was the problem with the qualifier system: it was essentially a second national league thrown into the middle of the championship, which was why people were voting with their feet. A structure which turned off the Mayo fans, football's most loyal and enthusiastic supporters, had something seriously wrong with it.

Some of the Mayo faithful might have feared a repeat of the previous year's mismatch. Dublin had scored fourteen goals in five matches to Mayo's four. In the qualifiers they'd had twelve points to spare over a Roscommon team Mayo scraped past by two. In their previous game they'd scored 5–17 against Cavan, the biggest score anyone hit all summer on Irish soil (Galway put up 5–21 against London in Ruislip). The reigning champions looked better than they had when winning the previous year's championship and quite a few people wondered if 2021 and 2022, when they lost semi-finals to Mayo in extra-time and Kerry by a point respectively, had just been a brief weird interregnum. Maybe normal service was now being restored and we were at the beginning of another six in a row. The gloomy prognosis about the impossibility of competing with metropolitan demographic and financial strength might prove true after all.

The speed with which they moved and the precise intricacy of their attacking patterns in the opening minutes showed why they'd blown so many teams away. No one flowed like Dublin in full spate. But Tommy Conroy sounded an early note of defiance with one of his trademark points, the top-speed gallop followed by the fisted finish, and at half-time the favourites were just one point ahead.

This had been the pattern of all the great games between the teams during the previous decade which made their rivalry into football's most enthralling. Dublin always seemed on the verge of pulling away but Mayo somehow stuck with them. At Dublin's peak under Jim Gavin Mayo were the only team that could do this. They'd been caricatured as bottlers for losing the 2013, 2016 and 2017 finals by a point to the Dubs but perhaps this was getting things backwards. Dublin were expected to win those games by several points. Mayo's fighting spirit and ability to rise to the occasion were what rendered those matches so nerve-wrackingly close. Having their defeats portrayed as stemming from psychological weakness seemed a poor reward.

They kept coming back and winning big games. They failed to win the biggest one of all because their way was barred by the greatest team of all time. Their performance in the 2017 final was probably the finest losing display in championship history. It was hard to see what more they could have done. It's probable that, as is the case with the Dutch teams which lost the 1974 and 1978 World Cup finals, posterity will be very kind to the reputation of that Mayo side and they'll be remembered long after many teams that actually achieved the ultimate triumph. Lee Keegan, Keith Higgins, Colm Boyle and Andy Moran were losers? Get away out of that.

His old team-mates had retired but Aidan O'Shea motored on. That day in Roscommon he was setting a championship record for outfield appearances. It had been an honourable career yet some opposition fans and the odd pundit had developed a set against the big man. Describing him as a hate figure would be too strong but he was certainly the object of undeserved derision from certain quarters. It was hard to explain why. Bêtes noires tended to be hard men with a notch of opposition scalps on their belt. O'Shea was much more sinned against than sinning in this regard. There'd been a couple of games against Dublin when referees had turned a blind eye to the spoiling tactics of a defence utterly panicked by his size and power at full-forward. No player had been fouled with impunity more often. O'Shea just got on with things, didn't bemoan his lot to the media and did his best to free himself of the defensive shackles.

A walking compendium of traditional football virtues with his high fielding, accurate kicking and physical strength, O'Shea occasionally seemed like a man out of time. You could imagine him being unstoppable back in the catch-and-kick era when midfielders nobly sought to outfield each other, with breaking the ball viewed as a dishonourable tactic. Instead he'd spent a career soaring to make high catches only to find himself belaboured by multiple opponents on returning to Earth. Small nippy forwards might seem the most obvious victims of the cynical play strangling the game like Japanese knotweed. But a small guy has some chance of getting sympathy from a ref. It's hard not to give a free to someone who's been sent flying. Big guys like O'Shea, and this was becoming David Clifford's problem as well, were expected to shrug off the cheap shots and keep going. It was like they were viewed as provoking the defenders by being that size.

Some of the animus against O'Shea seemed to stem from the belief that he was that old Irish bogeyman, the-man-who-thinks-he's-great. Yet there was no evidence for that contention.

There were players who gave interviews which dripped with self-regard, showboated on the field or taunted the opposition, but O'Shea wasn't one of them. Perhaps the problem was simply that he stood out by virtue of his physique and always gave the impression of enjoying both life and football. A certain Irish puritanism of spirit, described by John McGahern as the belief that it's morally good to be going around with a long face, hasn't entirely gone away.

O'Shea had won a Connacht title with Mayo in 2009. Other members of that team had gone on to become inter-county managers (Andy Moran, with Leitrim), CEO of the Gaelic Players Association (Tom Parsons) or minister of state with responsibility for local government and planning (Alan Dillon). O'Shea kept on keeping on. At thirty-three he wasn't the force of old but, on this record-breaking day, he produced his best display in years. Winning ball, distributing it wisely and generally directing the Mayo attack, he did more than anyone to help them stay in the game.

As the second half wore on Dublin would go a couple of points clear and seem on the verge of pulling away. Then Mayo would reduce the lead or draw level. Dublin flowed and Mayo grafted. The contrast between the teams was epitomised by the two star forwards who ended up joint top scorers with seven points each.

Dublin's Cormac Costello was an elegant footballer who seemed to glide across the ground at top speed and struck the ball over the bar with little apparent effort. He gave the impression of someone to whom football came naturally. Everything he did looked easy. Mayo star Ryan O'Donoghue's style was frantically busy by comparison. Whereas Costello had been an outstanding minor hurler, O'Donoghue's other sport was boxing where he'd been a national schoolboy champion. The sport seemed to have left its mark on him in the slightly crouched stance he adopted when in possession and in a determination to battle for every scrap. Costello seemed to float above the fray, O'Donoghue plunged into the thick of it. When he struck the ball, it was with a mighty swing of the boot. Everything he did looked effortful.

Early in the first half O'Donoghue looked through on goal before Brian Fenton, another supremely elegant Dub, cruised back to execute a block which reduced him to an uncoordinated tangle of limbs on the ground. There seemed a note of aristocratic disdain in the intervention. An incensed Mayo man in front of me booed in a very strange way. He didn't do a booing sound but shouted the word 'boo' over and over. Costello and O'Donoghue seemed like archetypal figures, the city slicker and the country boy. Both brilliant forwards, they skinned the cat in different ways.

The nearer we got to the end, the more you detected unease among the Dublin fans, who wondered why their team hadn't put the game away yet, and expectation from the Mayo fans, who sensed the possibility of a famous upset. With eleven minutes left and the teams level, a superb Costello pass put Eoin Murchan galloping through the middle. Murchan's shot left goalkeeper Colm Reape helpless but it struck the crossbar and flew over.

Dublin were still a point up entering injury-time when referee Martin McNally did Mayo a couple of favours. First he gave them a 45 which definitely shouldn't have been a 45 and Reape sauntered upfield to stick it over the bar. Then he gave them a free which probably shouldn't have been a free and O'Donoghue landed that one too.

Mayo fans were on their feet all over the ground, Mr Boo among them. He turned round to see if he could enhance his pleasure by sticking it to a nearby Dublin fan. None being available, he leaped out into the aisle to shake a fist at an imaginary one. There were thirty seconds left – all Mayo had to do was win the kick-out or, failing that, hold Dublin up inside their own half.

Stephen Cluxton gambled by going long to the right wing and as the ball travelled half the length of the pitch two Mayo men were in pole position to claim it. Then Ciarán Kilkenny came back the field, jumped over both of them, caught the ball and on landing slipped a pass to Jack McCaffrey. There were plenty of quick players in Gaelic football but Dublin's wing-back was on another plane altogether. A supersonic one. In full flight he made you think that someone had used a camera trick to speed up his personal film. The most appropriate comparison seemed less with another player than with Road Runner, Speedy Gonzales and other animated speed merchants.

McCaffrey beep-beeped over the half-way line, Mayo players filling the Wile E. Coyote and Sylvester the Cat roles in hot pursuit. On the way out afterwards Mayo fans lamented the failure to bring the flying doctor to ground at this stage. 'Other counties would have fouled him,' they moaned. In truth Mayo's problem wasn't an excess of the Corinthian spirit. They'd have rugby-tackled McCaffrey if they'd caught him. But they couldn't catch him so on he flew, playing a one-two with Colm Basquel before setting up Costello for what should have been an easy equaliser. Costello lost his footing but as the defenders closed in he clambered to his feet and, after switching the ball to his left hand to avoid being blocked, fisted the equaliser over the bar. Seconds later it was all over. Another Houdini act from the Dubs, another addition to that bulkiest of all Irish sporting volumes, Mayo-might-have-beens.

It was the best football match of the season, good enough to prompt a few optimistic souls into suggesting maybe the game wasn't in rag order after all. Except Dublin–Mayo was actually the exception which proved just how bad the rule was. It wasn't an alibi for the rest of the football championship but an indictment of it. That last-gasp Dublin attack, with its great catch, its slick passing, its blistering solo run, its improvisation in front of goal, showed just how good Gaelic football could be and how talented its players were when released from the prevailing negativity. They had the ability to do thrilling things but weren't getting the chance anymore. One Hyde Park swallow would not save football's summer of discontent.

Six days later Mayo were held to a draw by Derry in a scrappy preliminary quarter-final and lost on penalties. That Mayo, who had lost one game by a single injury-time point, were out while Derry, who'd lost three by a total of twenty-two points, were still in proved the stupendous illogicality of the ridiculous championship structure. Perhaps the big effort Mayo had put in six days previously during a game played at a much higher pace than most qualifier matches told on them. Maybe another last-gasp disappointment had taken a psychological toll.

At this remove they seem like the unluckiest team of the 2024 championship. It took a wonder kick by Connor Gleeson to defeat them in the Connacht final and a wonder score by Dublin to deny them victory in Roscommon. Had they won either of those games Mayo might have gone very close to winning that elusive All-Ireland. The initial reaction to their earlyish exit was that their manager's confidence had been ill-founded. On mature reflection McStay was right, Mayo really weren't far off the pace. 2024 might even have been another one that got away.

It's also possible that the team damaged most by Costello's equaliser was not Mayo but Dublin. Jim Gavin's six-in-a-row team had an unprecedented ability to squeeze out victories in tight finishes. Two of that sextet were won by one point, as was the 2013 final two years before the unbroken run began. That made three single-point wins in seven years, an anomalous figure considering there'd been just two in the nineties, one in the noughties and none at all in the seventies.

Dublin's two-point All-Ireland final victory the previous year added to the mystique. The way they'd swept upfield to equalise in Roscommon suggested they could get out of anything. Perhaps they'd started to subconsciously feel that way themselves. There'd been a slight air of complacency about their performance against Mayo, a suggestion of a team playing within themselves who knew they could turn it on when the going got tough. All summer the conventional wisdom was that Dublin and Kerry 'had plenty left in the tank'. When push came to shove the tank was where it stayed. Had Mayo won by a point the shock might have done the champions good in the long run. We could have ended up with another Dublin–Mayo All-Ireland final.

'Six pints for breakfast,' said the Dublin fan gleefully on the platform at Roscommon station the next morning.

'I was grand till you said to get that Cointreau,' said his friend and shook his head.

There was six of them, aged somewhere between forty and sixty, and in the high good humour of hungover men who'd located an early house.

'I thought we hated Mayo till we came to Roscommon. They're obsessed with it.'

'The oul lady coming with the paper, "Mayo drew Derry," she says and smiles.'

'A fiver a pint. They don't rob you. Remember that place in Cork, seven fifty.'

'That was seven in the morning. You'd have paid a grand.'

The boisterous laughter of people who enjoy each other's company unreservedly rang through the station.

'It's a long time. 1996. A long time together. Hey, I know you, don't I?'

The passing Dub who'd just been hailed told them he worked in an inner-city pub.

'Doing what?'

'Pulling pints.'

'It's people from Drimnagh that has that, isn't it? Boxing crowd.'

The circle widened to accommodate this fellow stranger in a strange land. A couple of girls in school uniform passed by. The tone switched to an awkward courtliness, as though the men were reminded of daughters at home past and present.

'Are yiz on the mitch, girls?'

'No, we're on a study day. We're doing the Leaving.'

'How is it going so far?'

'Alright. We have one subject left.'

'Best of luck, girls.'

There was a visible relaxation as the scholars proceeded down the platform.

'Did you see Kilkenny catching the ball? He nearly jumped out into the graveyard.'

'The crossbar is still rattling this morning from Murchan's shot.'

'That ref should never get a game again.'

'There was a Mayo guy talking filth in front of kids behind the goal. A fella went over and asked him to stop. He wouldn't stop so your man loafed him.'

'Hate that, fellas talking filth in front of kids. Not right.'

'There's a friend of mine, he's seventy years old. A young Mayo lad was squaring up to him and he says, "If you hit one Dub, you hit 10,000 of us."'

'It's great to be travelling. It's great to be together.'

'You'll be tired by the time you make it back to Wexford.'

'I'll sleep all the way down.'

The train pulled in, and as they made their slightly unsteady way on board, one of the magnificent seven turned to me, flashed a red-faced grin and said, 'Fair play to yiz. Yiz hate Mayo even more than we do.'

I could have explained that I wasn't from Roscommon but sometimes you just have to take a compliment in the spirit it's given.

15

The Teacher and the Microbiologist

THE WOMAN AT THE DELI COUNTER IN SUPERVALU
thought it was a bad idea, the woman at the checkout thought
it was a bad idea, Chris O'Brien the caretaker at the community
school who was getting the trophies won by its ladies' football
team engraved thought it was a bad idea. Why was an All-
Ireland hurling quarter-final starting at a quarter past one on a
Saturday afternoon?

It was because RTÉ and the GAA had both given other
sports priority over hurling. RTÉ thought the final of the United
Rugby Championship was more important so hurling had to be
out of the way before the egg-chasers went into action. Why
had the hurling been scheduled for Saturday in the first place?
Because the GAA shifted it there so the semi-finals of the

Tailteann Cup, the competition for second-tier football teams, could take prime position on the Sunday.

RTÉ's priorities looked even more skewed when the Munster–Leinster decider they'd presumably anticipated didn't materialise. The hurling quarter-finals ended up playing second fiddle to the meeting of perennial Irish audience favourites Northern Transvaal Bulls and Glasgow Warriors.

Most of the responsibility for the fiasco lay with the GAA who, to coax Congress delegates into approving a two-tier football championship, guaranteed prime-time RTÉ coverage for the second-level competition. Hence the presence of two second-class football matches in the top broadcast slots while 40 per cent of the hurling championship's remaining matches were relegated to Saturday.

It made no sense that this Croke Park Sunday would be reserved for the Tailteann Cup semis. The actual final, which the uninitiated might regard as more important, would be a curtain-raiser to an All-Ireland semi-final on a Saturday afternoon. The GAA may have fantasised that the counties involved in the Tailteann Cup, seeing it as their All-Ireland, would flock to Croke Park in their droves. Instead Down, Sligo, Laois and Kildare between them pulled in a grand total of 10,348 fans. The hurling quarter-finals drew 30,509 and that 3:1 ratio in their favour considerably understates the disparity in national interest.

Why didn't RTÉ say to the GAA, 'We can't show these

Tailteann Cup semis on the Sunday. Nobody cares, they're not big matches.' Indeed why were the GAA able to guarantee national TV coverage for the competition to sway wavering delegates? It's not actually a national TV station. The answer is that RTÉ was doing its commercial partner a favour and putting the licence-payers' interests second to those of the GAA. It was public service broadcasting but not as we know it.

Jarlath Burns seemed to realise how bad this all looked and made a last-ditch effort to switch the quarter-finals to Sunday and the Tailteann Cup games to Saturday. He'd have got away with it too if it hadn't been for Seán Carroll. The chairman of Sligo County Board decided that, having been promised Sunday all along, his county weren't going to be denied it at the last minute. He rallied sufficient Central Council delegates to kill Burns' proposal.

I couldn't help feeling parochial pride in the small-county bloody-mindedness displayed by my fellow Sligoman. Sligo hadn't created the problem and they didn't see why they should have to fix it. It had the authentic 'I wouldn't give them the satisfaction' rural note. Carroll's All-Star revolt was a triumph for GAA democracy. Burns had shown leadership by trying to change matters but the fact he couldn't impose that leadership by fiat was a good thing. Cork's game with Dublin stayed at a quarter past one.

A certain mutinous air pervaded Thurles that Saturday lunch-time, a sensation of supporters being present under protest. The vibe was wrong and vibes matter. I'd been in Dublin the night before and went down to Thurles on the train from Heuston. The carriage was still almost all Cork supporters but the sole Dublin fan dominated proceedings.

Perhaps a few years younger than me, he had a ginger moustache and a voice like the boring priest from *Father Ted* who goes on about running the electricity off the gas. He'd become fixated by a couple in their twenties named Darren and Ellie and plied them with questions about their lives and their relationships.

'Darren, what did Ellie wear to the debs?'

'I don't know, we weren't going out then.'

'Ah. Ellie, what did the fella you went to the debs with wear?'

'A dark suit.'

'Did he look better now in a dark suit than Darren would have looked in a dark suit?'

'Ellie, when Darren would be drunk would you prefer if he got violent or if he was just stupid and messing around?'

He couldn't have made the carriage more uneasy if he'd produced a machete. The nature of the interrogation had everyone on tenterhooks waiting for it to slip over the boundary into the unacceptable. What made it so excruciatingly embarrassing was that both Darren and Ellie were incredibly polite and answered every one of the questions. For the record she would prefer him to be stupid and messing around than violent. A woman opposite me stared into her book as though pondering an escape by tunnelling through the pages. It felt like we were the subject of a prank. Your man would whip off the false tash, reveal that he was Mike Murphy from *The Live Mike* and point out where the camera had been hidden.

'I was in a hotel once and they threw me out for cheering when someone dropped a glass. Darren, if someone dropped a glass would you cheer and say good luck or would you just say nothing?'

'I suppose I wouldn't say anything.'

'Ellie, if someone dropped a glass would you cheer and say good luck or would you just say nothing?'

Some Trans-Siberian Express journeys probably didn't feel this long. The insistent quality of the guy's voice prevented anyone else from starting a conversation. When he went to the jacks there was a huge collective sigh of relief. Literally. It was audible.

'You poor things,' said the woman with the book. 'I honestly thought you'd get off at the last station and get a taxi to Thurles.'

It had crossed my mind too. For myself. On his way back your man stopped by a seat with four young lads, one wearing a Kilkenny jersey.

'Are ye going to the match, lads?'

'We're from Kilkenny. We don't do quarter-finals. Hahoooo.'

'Do you know what I say, do you know what I say when I meet people from Kilkenny? I say "Miaaaaaowwwwww".'

It was the most blood-curdling feline moment since Taylor

Swift's appearance in *Cats*. He trotted back to his seat and all was blissfully silent for a minute.

'Kilkenny. The Cats. Ellie, do you have a cat?'

As we left the station I watched him gaze round in puzzlement as though looking for someone. Further ahead Darren and Ellie, Ireland's best-mannered couple, weaved through the crowds at high speed. They deserved a good afternoon.

Outside Semple Stadium someone had set up a wooden board covered with pictures of GAA personalities. The pictures had holes cut in them. Put a sliotar through one of the holes and you'd win a cash prize. I think it was ten euros for Brian Cody and twenty for Marty Morrissey. A line of small kids with their own hurls queued up to try their luck. All struck the ball well enough to make you marvel at how quickly kids in hurling counties master the skills. Balls missed by inches and came back off the rim, the youngsters' expressions as fiercely determined as those of any penalty-taker in an All-Ireland final. Quite a crowd gathered to watch the contest. It was nearly the best thing we saw that afternoon.

After their dismemberment by Kilkenny, Dublin must have feared something similar from a Cork team which had run so rampant on its previous visit to Thurles. The cautious quality of their play suggested as much. But there was something slightly off about Cork. The vibe wasn't right about them either. It might have been a come-down from the emotional highs of the Limerick and Tipperary victories because they hadn't been great against Offaly in the previous week's preliminary quarter-final either.

The match was like a Russian election. Everyone knew who was going to win but the formalities still had to be gone through. There were incidental pleasures — Patrick Horgan and Declan Dalton hit nice points for Cork, Dublin midfielder Conor Burke, who'd mounted a one-man resistance campaign in the Leinster final, landed three good ones — but the game never got going. Not just the Cork players but the Cork fans failed to rise to the height of previous days. The Rebels were five up by the end of the first half and nine clear seven minutes into the second. This game was dead only to wash it.

All remaining excitement was packed into the final five minutes as Dublin, finally realising a lacklustre Cork weren't going to administer a trouncing, pressed forward and created three good goal chances. Had any gone in maybe we'd have had a grandstand finish. It's more likely Cork would have been roused from their slumber and retaliated with three points or a goal of their own. The Rebels won by five in the end but what glory there was to be extracted from this underwhelming match went to Dublin. Their strong finish and refusal to crumble redeemed much of the honour lost in their crushing by Kilkenny.

The Dublin spirit was encapsulated by Eoghan O'Donnell.

One of the best full-backs in the game, O'Donnell had been infected by the general malaise as Dublin's defence fell to bits in the Leinster final. In Thurles he completely shackled goal machine Alan Connolly and inspired his team's late flurry with a great foray up the field which almost brought a goal.

Connolly wasn't the only Cork man brought back to reality with a bump that lunchtime. In the heady aftermath of the trouncing of Tipperary it seemed that Cork posed a serious threat to Limerick's five-in-a-row hopes. The afternoon's struggles, coupled with the champions' recent performances, made that prognosis seem optimistic. Maybe we'd all got a bit carried away.

Dublin weren't the only team seeking to recover from a disappointing provincial final. Two weeks previously Limerick had beaten Clare in the Munster decider for the third successive year. Expectations had been sky-high going into the match after two previous epics. In 2022 Limerick needed extra-time before winning by three points; in 2023 they won by one. The Banner gave Limerick more trouble than anyone else, drawing with them in the 2021 round robin game and beating them a year later. This time round Limerick had six points to spare. The ease of that victory prompted speculation that Clare's big chance had gone.

It was one way of looking at it. The other was that the massive efforts Clare had delivered in previous finals contributed to subsequent All-Ireland semi-final defeats by Kilkenny. They'd left almost everything in Thurles. This time they'd departed Semple Stadium without firing all their shots. It might stand to them in the long term.

This was a minority view. There were even predictions that Clare might lose to a Wexford team who'd beaten Galway by eight points and given Brian Lohan's team a serious fright two years previously.

It looked pretty routine for Clare when they moved 0–12 to 0–5 clear by the twenty-fourth minute but Wexford rallied to hit 1–4 without reply in six minutes. The stage seemed set for an enthralling contest but this appealing vista disappeared as suddenly as it had materialised. Rory O'Connor had been the central figure in Wexford's comeback. He'd been fouled for the penalty from which Lee Chin scored their goal and produced a couple of blistering runs which electrified his team-mates. He was also the central figure in their demise, inflicting a late chop on David Reidy which saw him receive a second yellow card after thirty-two minutes. All hope of an upset vanished in that moment.

A brace of quick points left Clare two up at the break. A terrific goal in the forty-fourth minute put them six clear and confirmed that Wexford's resistance would be futile. The points and the goal came from perhaps the two most interesting hurlers in the championship, both of whom would play central roles in the All-Ireland final.

The point-scorer, Tony Kelly, was the most gifted hurler of

his generation and one of the most gifted there'd ever been. His greatness had been obvious since 2013 when he became the first player, and only the second to date, to win both Hurler and Young Hurler of the Year awards when Clare won a surprise All-Ireland. Some undistinguished years followed as the team seemed affected by the *I, Claudius* levels of infighting and backstabbing within the county but Kelly maintained his reputation as one of the game's finest forwards.

As the twenties dawned he went into overdrive. It began in the belated crowd-free Covid-haunted championship season of 2020 when, though his team were well beaten by Limerick, Kelly landed seventeen points, eight from play. 0–13 against Laois and 1–15 against Wexford, 0–6 from play, followed before Waterford eliminated Clare from the truncated competition. It was a sustained burst of scoring with few analogues. 2021 brought more big tallies before he produced one of the great Munster campaigns the following year. Ten points, four from play, helped Clare to a narrow win over Cork before he bagged five from play against the notably mean Limerick defence in a round robin draw. In the Munster final a forewarned Limerick found him even more irresistible as he shot seven points from play in possibly the finest performance of his career. In 2023 he'd hit 1–4 from play against Cork and 3–4 from play against Dublin.

Quantity was matched by quality. Kelly seemed to have a higher proportion of unlikely scores to his belt than any other forward, steered over from impossible angles, under the severest of pressure, snapped up in the blink of an eye thanks to a dexterity which made the hurl look as easily manipulable as a table-tennis bat. His striking possessed a beautiful economy which made sending the ball seventy yards with a flick of the wrist look like something anyone could manage. Above all there was an exhilarating freedom about the way he played, floating around the attack, drifting back towards midfield or into his own half-back line, swooping on a loose ball and soloing at speed down the sideline before pulling the trigger, which suggested a relish for the game's capacity for self-expression. Kelly's play constituted the best possible argument for hurling as an art form. His style, like the music of Willie Clancy, Bobby Casey, Tony MacMahon and Micho Russell, was imbued with the joy of life.

No one was more fun to watch because no one gave the same impression of doing things off the cuff for the hell of it. But perhaps this instinctive approach contributed to the unpredictability which sometimes bedevilled Kelly in the biggest games. There were days when he just didn't seem to be feeling it and the game entirely passed him by as though he 'didn't be well', in a hurling sense. Two All-Ireland semi-finals against Kilkenny, in which he'd scored a combined total of one point from play, were prime examples. In the 2022 final Kelly's eclipse at the hands of rookie Kilkenny corner-back Mikey Butler seemed to demoralise his team-mates as they slumped to a heavy defeat. Clare, everyone agreed, depended too much on Tony Kelly. That was why news he'd miss some of the round robin stage through injury appeared to bode ill for their qualification chances.

Instead they'd made the Munster final without him. It wasn't till the final that Kelly finally started. Clare had learned to cope without him. Restored to the team, their erstwhile main man had the chance to be the jewel in the crown rather than the whole enchilada.

In Kelly's absence, the post of attack leader had passed to Shane O'Donnell. O'Donnell had also made his name in 2013, with a final replay hat-trick of goals which made a media sensation, *Late Late Show* and all, out of the tousle-haired full-forward who looked like he was on secondment from a boy band. If Kelly had a job which seemed archetypally inter-county player, teaching in the great hurling nursery of St Flannan's, Ennis, where he coached the senior team, his team-mate's calling was a more exotic one. A brilliant student, O'Donnell had attended Harvard on a prestigious Fulbright scholarship before returning to UCC to complete a PhD in microbiology. He had ambitions to become a researcher on the International Space Station, 'to try and understand how microbiomes survive in zero gravity, how different organisms survive and thrive in zero gravity environments. That's something that ties very nicely with research that I did'. His devotion to science even extended to having the chemical formula for adrenaline tattooed on his right arm. One of my daughters describes this as 'badass'. Though, as a student of biology at Imperial College, London, she may not be entirely neutral on such matters.

O'Donnell's introductory inter-county salvo turned out to be misleading. He was more score-maker than score-taker. A combination of speed, touch, intelligence and incredible aerial ability for a man of his size helped him become one of hurling's finest target men. Had the sport kept a list of assists over the previous decade, he'd have been near the top. His greatest asset of all was a bravery which saw him hurtle towards any incoming ball at speed no matter how many defenders were doing likewise. It was the kind of instinctive courage which appears to refuse the possibility of injury.

Yet three years previously he'd suffered a concussion during a Clare training session which took both a physical and a psychological toll on him. A year later he told a medical conference on concussion in sport hosted by the UCD School of Medicine how in the aftermath of the injury he'd suffered prolonged spells of nausea and a feeling of pressure in his head which made him consider giving up sport altogether.

The migraines were accompanied by mounting anxiety. Three months later when O'Donnell got what he described as 'a pretty innocuous bang' on the head he became convinced that he'd been concussed again. 'The power of the mind was insane that I had all the symptoms again,' he remembered.

After discussing it with his doctor, O'Donnell concluded that he hadn't been concussed, but that the fear of concussion made him think he had been. A clinical psychologist, Niamh Willis, suggested that he was suffering from a form of post-traumatic stress disorder. As O'Donnell's girlfriend, she seemed in a good position to make the diagnosis. He spoke with great honesty about how disorientating it felt, as someone for whom science, rationality and intelligence were central, to be affected in this way.

O'Donnell's experience struck chords with me. Fear triggering the very thing it feared. The feeling of your mind turning against you. The temptation to give up and throw everything away. The realisation that you weren't as strong as you'd imagined. I'd never been concussed, played inter-county hurling or been noted for my courage but O'Donnell's comeback was one of the examples which helped as I took my own faltering steps back on to the field of normal everyday life. Of course it didn't take him two decades to seek help. But seeing him back braving the blows the way he always had done was a boost to my morale, a proof that there was a way out, a sign that there was no shame in falling prey to anxiety because it could happen to the strongest of us. No one could call this man a wimp. It helped to hear his story.

O'Donnell was a very impressive character all round. Two days before picking up the Hurler of the Year award that October, he declared his objection to having his picture used to promote GAAGO. He disagreed with the idea of GAAGO, which he described as 'a not particularly popular initiative'. 'The GAA should be swallowing the cost of promoting the game and paying to televise these games,' he argued.

His role as creator rather than finisher sometimes resulted in O'Donnell being under-rated. He'd never been a prolific scorer but in 2024 he amassed the biggest championship total of his career and became the complete attacking package.

Eight minutes into the second half against Wexford, he collected the ball sixty yards from the opposition goal, shook off repeated attempts by a defender to drag him down, beat another by dummying to shoot for a point but hopping the ball on his hurl instead, hopped it once more to make space and finished with a volley past a wrong-footed goalie. It was ruthless and so was the way Clare put Wexford to the sword in the second half as they finished with a twelve-point margin. The extra man had been a help but the Banner's impressive sharpness suggested it would be foolish to dismiss their chances even if they were being treated as an afterthought.

There was a surprising number of gardaí around as the Cork fans made their way towards the train. There was even one on horseback though the effect was somewhat spoiled when the horse leaned over the wall of a house near the station for a woman to rub his head and to take up a little girl's offer of sweets. The supporters were being herded into a line with what seemed like slightly excessive zeal. One guy was being taken out of the queue as I arrived.

'When am I going to get on the train?'

'If you don't do anything wrong, you'll get on the train.'

A little guy with a tash turned to me and said angrily, 'They don't do themselves any favours, do they?'

He was with two other lads, a bigger guy with a bushier tash and a tall blond lad who might have passed for a model but for the pitted skin on his jaw. They'd had a few pints, were fuming with a sense of injustice and stared down the guards as though contemplating an attack. The guards for their part seemed to be paying the trio special attention. The tension in the air contrasted with the soporific nature of the games. A couple of younger guys pointed out a friend of theirs who'd eschewed joining the line and stood next to a bin throwing back cans like a thirsty seventies kid necking small bottles of Cadet Cola.

'He has the right idea. We should have done the same thing,' one of them said in the admiring tone of a businessman applauding a wise investment.

After all the kerfuffle at the station the most eventful thing on the journey home was a group of women singing 'The Rattlin' Bog' at lightning speed. After a few drinks there's a great danger that the nest will end up on the bird and the twig will land in the bog but they managed admirably.

Getting off in Cork, the male model was talking amicably to a woman with a small child. The big lad with the tash burst into the station toilets and addressed the micturating throng: 'It smells like half past two in here, boys. It smells like half past two.' He repeated it with great glee and though no one knew exactly what the phrase meant it seemed to capture the spirit of the hour.

It had been a half past two kind of day. Even if it started at a quarter past one.

16

A Matter of Life and Death

THERE'S NO ESCAPING THE GAA.

After they'd flung the last shovelfuls of earth over my uncle's coffin a few days after the hurling quarter-finals, two of the gravedigging party walked over to me. 'Eamonn,' said one of them, 'have you met Cillian? He's on the Galway panel.'

My Uncle Páraic would probably have appreciated that encounter. Death got him in the end but he met it on his own terms. He'd fought back from the brink and got out of hospital a couple of months earlier. When he died it was peacefully in his own bed at home.

A few years previously I'd met an acquaintance of his from the greyhound racing world. They'd served on Bord na gCon together. 'Páraic Feeney,' he said when I disclosed the familial relationship, 'a nice man.' It perfectly captured my uncle's personality. Niceness defined him.

A nice man is no small thing to be. I try my best but it's not always easy. It doesn't come entirely naturally. Niceness, regrettably, is neither my factory setting nor my default mode. I try but that's how it is for some of us. Some people are unaffectedly and effortlessly nice. It's just in their character. They can't help it, they were born that way. They're the people you've never heard say a bad word about anyone. That's quite the achievement when you think about our national record in this field. As Dr Johnson said, 'The Irish are a fair people. They never speak well of one another.'

Páraic's niceness comes across in the opening pages of the American film critic Joseph McBride's definitive biography of John Ford where he helps the writer out as he seeks the family background of our illustrious distant relation. The Ford connection also led to an utterly unexpected online encounter. A film entitled *Innisfree* by the great Spanish documentary-maker Jose Luis Guerin, about his obsession with *The Quiet Man*, made a list of best Spanish movies ever in a poll organised by the magazine *Caimán Cuadernos de Cine*. After tracking it down online I saw in the opening frames my uncles Páraic and Bartley speaking their native language in the ruins of the house where Ford's father was born. They seemed to me, as they did when I was a kid, like repositories of age and wisdom, though Bartley is the same age I am now and Páraic over a decade younger.

This immortality is ironic for a man who brought diffidence to a fine art. But he'll be there forever with his brother in the Iberian cinematic canon, wearing a tweed cap and looking thoughtfully at the limestone walls. A short while later he walks across the graveyard where thirty-four years on he'll be buried, kneels by a headstone of a long-deceased Feeney and prays, 'Go ndéanfaidh Dia trócaire air a anam.' A few seconds later the Spanish subtitles read, *Todos muerto, Muertos.*

Páraic and Bartley's appearance in the film, I tell the congregation at the funeral where his daughter Máiréad had asked me to say a few words, is an example of the old movie trick of attracting the audience by blatant displays of sex appeal.

We're not supposed to have favourites among our children. Does the same hold for other relatives? No matter. Páraic was my favourite uncle. We'd bonded early over a love of sport. I remember one scorching summer day when everyone else was out doing wholesome things in the sun and we sweltered in the living room of his house listening to the famous 1979 Leinster semi-final between Dublin and Offaly, the former's comeback soon to be immortalised by future Electric Picnic favourites The Wolfe Tones in the song 'Fourteen Men'.

Like any good country lad, reared on perhaps apocryphal tales of Dublin's villainous sledging of rural opposition – 'Did you feed the pigs this morning?'; 'I can see the welly marks on the back of your legs' – I was rooting passionately against the city slickers. Páraic, to my disappointment, took their side perhaps because his wife Moya was from Swords and he'd lived in Dublin, first sharing a flat with my mother who was in the civil service, living later in Portmarnock while working as a draughtsman with Dublin Corporation. He eventually moved to work with Galway County Council, where he attained a senior position in the planning department, and built a house less than a mile from where he'd been born, fifty yards from where Bartley, his Spanish co-star, had done the same.

We shared a love not just of the games but of the facts and figures, the minutiae and the trivia attached to them. He may have suspected my eventual career path long before anyone else did. Including myself. A walking Wikipedia *avant la lettre*, he'd gently test my familiarity with the more esoteric, obscure and arcane corners of sporting knowledge. Then I'd test him back.

As we both got older we'd jointly visit the memory palace where games and players and goals and points and saves were stored. One of the highlights of any visit to Spiddal would be his arrival to the house where for a few hours we'd briefly run through the sporting controversies of the day before going back in time together. In the last few years when Parkinson's disease had ended his driving, Máiréad would drop him up.

It was harder to think of Páraic having left the world than of anyone else I could remember. My cousin Éanna spoke about his father's love of sport at the start of the funeral service and mentioned how Páraic read my stuff in the papers. Most people have an 'ideal reader' in mind when they write. My Uncle Páraic was mine. Nothing pleased me more than learning from my mother when he thought I'd got it right. He said nothing on the occasions I got it wrong. He was too nice.

My mother and Páraic as second youngest and youngest had been close. She'd always felt protective towards him. At the age of twelve he'd spent a year in hospital with TB and even received the last rites. At that time and place children died of illness more frequently than they do now. One of my mother's friends had died during a diphtheria epidemic, which saw the Coláiste Chonnacht Irish college turned into an emergency hospital.

Páraic had lived to have children and grandchildren, of whom he was very proud. As we sat down for the meal in the Connemara Coast Hotel the latter tore around the corridor outside the dining room, oblivious to the sombre atmosphere. It was a welcome interjection. In the midst of death we were in life.

I wondered how my mother felt after burying two sisters and two brothers. The Feeney Survival Stakes was now a two-horse race between herself and Bartley who, though he had several years, start on her, seemed indestructible. In his ninetieth year he'd chased down a young man who'd skipped out of his B&B without paying.

A man at my table told me he'd played minor football with Galway, along with Tommy Joe Gilmore, my very first football hero, for a famous solo point in their 1973 All-Ireland senior final defeat by Cork. He presumed I'd heard of the famous Menlough–Spiddal controversy. I hadn't so he filled me in. Back in the seventies he'd played for Menlough when they beat Spiddal in a county junior football semi-final. Spiddal learned that a Menlough player had played a club match in another county the same year and launched an objection. Menlough put in a counter-objection. 'They ruled against us. The meeting was in a hotel in Athenry and we wrecked the place. We took a trophy off the table and threw it at the county chairman. *The Irish Press* ran a piece on it, "All this trouble over a junior match".' It resembled one of the great tales of mayhem from Breandán Ó hEithir's memoir *Over the Bar* and novel *Lead Us into Temptation*. The 'GAA man' gets as much pleasure from the stories as the games.

'Do you really think Galway will beat Dublin on Saturday?' he asked me.

'Ah no. Not really.'

I'd finished my eulogy for Páraic by saying it was a pity he wouldn't be around to see Galway beat Dublin in Croke Park the following Saturday. It was a laugh line and received as such. Galway hadn't beaten Dublin in the championship since 1934.

But Galway did beat Dublin. Four points up at half-time, three up with ten minutes to go, the Dubs appeared in control and set to close out the match in their usual manner. When Galway took the lead for the first time in the sixty-seventh minute Dublin seemed blind-sided. Galway went two up and though the champions pulled one back, Con O'Callaghan missed a chance which would have sent the game into extra-time. The result turned the championship on its head and put paid to the lingering traces of the Dublin invincibility myth. The narrow defeats of 2021 and 2022 had turned out to be not blips but harbingers of decline. Dublin were just another team now.

I have nothing else to say about this game. I'd hung on in Spiddal after the funeral and the match wasn't on RTÉ. It was on GAAGO but after so noisily opposing the streaming service I couldn't take advantage of it. My mother, who felt the same way, wouldn't use it either which meant our viewing of the match was restricted to a measly collection of RTÉ highlights. You can call this principle or you can call it thickness.

17

Atrocity Exhibition

IT WAS DUBLIN'S GREAT WEEKEND OF TAYLOR SWIFT. All trains to the capital from Galway were booked so I took the bus. Two girls in spectacular flowing white outfits waited till everyone else got off before alighting at Bachelors Walk. 'We don't want anyone stepping on these dresses.' Gaggles of laughing, singing Swifties floated and shimmered through the city streets, made and dressed up to the nines, a walking sunburst of glamour, excitement and good humour turning the city into a combination of catwalk and parade ground. This was their weekend. Even the championship was just a sideshow next to this.

The rainbows of Pride, whose weekend this had also been, were everywhere to be seen too. An American tourist congratulated the young woman at the hotel reception on their ubiquity. 'Thanks,' she said. 'We like to make a big deal of it here.'

Running late, I hailed my only taxi of the summer. The driver was a man in his sixties from Moldova whose immaculate suit and regal air made me feel like I was in a limousine. He told me he'd once been a mechanic with his own garage. After the disintegration of law and order which followed the collapse of the Soviet Union he was forced to pay protection money to gangsters. Suspecting they'd eventually kill him and take over the business, he'd scraped together the money for a visa and bought a one-way plane ticket to London. Changing planes at a German airport, he met some people he knew from home. They went to the bar and he ended up missing his connecting flight. You could go to Ireland instead, one of his friends suggested. Look, there's a flight going there in an hour.

That was twenty-three years ago. His kids had been brought up in Ireland. One of them had finished college and was out in Australia at the moment.

'I love this country. It's been good to me.'

His daughter, who'd done Irish in school, told him some of the words sounded like their equivalents in Moldovan. He wondered if there was a historic link between the two countries.

The taxi driver recommended that I visit Moldova and assured me that their wine, 'a beautiful golden wine', would be the next big thing in the world of viticulture. He loved the country but he wouldn't be going back.

'I don't mind Russians but they're never comfortable just living in another country. They have to try and take it over. Transnistria, Armenia, Azerbaijan, Ukraine. We're next on the list.'

Strolling towards Croke Park, I thought of his stories, how many others there must be like it in the country and in this city and how little I usually thought about them. The Immaculate Moldovan had started something.

'The funny thing is,' he'd said as I got out in Ballybough, 'that I've still never been to London.'

Donegal and Louth were starting the second half of the quarter-final as I took my seat. There was a whole lot of handpassing going on in the game. Louth's was of the familiar laboured variety but you could forgive the plodding nature of their football. Former Dublin player Ger Brennan had worked wonders to get them this far and any sight of a Louth jersey brought back memories of the 2010 Leinster football final when they'd been victims of the greatest robbery in GAA history, Meath's Joe Sheridan scoring a blatantly illegal last-gasp goal to deny them a first title in fifty-three years. The closest they'd come to a Leinster title since was their four-point defeat in this year's decider when, plucky and all as they'd been, they never for one second looked likely winners. Louth deserved an exemption from admonition.

You didn't need to make any allowances for Donegal. There seemed a pattern to the convolutions of their build-up. It was like they were actually executing complicated sequences of set moves. They'd pass and pass and pass and pass and eventually a free man would come in at the end of the move and stick the ball over the bar. Most frequently it was Footballer of the Year-elect Peadar Mogan, who finished with five points from play despite being named at corner-back, something which had probably never happened in Croke Park before. Donegal's backs would finish with 1–9 from play, outscoring an attack which hit 0–7. Their midfield chipped in with 0–5. It was a kind of 'total football' whose fluidity made Donegal, when on song, the game's most entertaining team that summer.

This was hardly what anyone had expected from McGuinness' return. It was as if Mr Kurtz had walked out of the jungle, shouted 'Hey, everyone, let's party', and led his army of tribesmen in an exuberant Bollywood dance number. Donegal had been the third-highest scorers in the group stages after Dublin and Kerry and the 1–23 they put up against Louth would be the highest tally in the knockout phase. Having spent his previous term seeing how far you could take defence, football's mad professor now seemed interested in discovering new dimensions to attack. Not everyone gets more conservative as they grow older.

This change of managerial personality spilled on to the field. Great and all as the Donegal 2013 team was, the players sometimes had the air of automatons rigidly following the pre-set programming for fear their creator might press their self-destruct button should the wrong move be made. Donegal 2024's status as the championship's happy warriors was summed up by the only goal of the game which arrived eleven minutes from time.

When Eoghan Bán Gallagher found Aaron Doherty just outside the square, the sub went all Harlem Globetrotters with an overhead flick towards Paddy McBrearty. McBrearty couldn't collect the ball but improvised by fisting the bouncing ball which struck the post and travelled all the way across the square, where Gallagher closed the circle by first-timing it to the net. It was a joyously chaotic score which left you with a 'Come on, lads, really?' grin on your face.

The handpass was often blamed for the laborious nature of modern football. Yet Donegal showed that the problem was not with the handpass per se but with the way it was employed. A spokesman for the handpass lobby might have used the slogan, 'Handpasses don't kill games, players kill games'. It ain't what you handpass, it's the way that you handpass. Donegal's Fun Boy Three of Gallagher, Doherty and McBrearty had shown how to do it.

The Donegal–Louth quarter-final was the first part of a double bill and the following pages will discuss the Kerry–Derry quarter-final. Trigger warning: Those of a sensitive disposition are advised to skip forward to the next chapter.

I'm not a cynic or a pessimist about Gaelic football. I'm a disappointed optimist who believes before every game that it might be great. I even had high hopes for Kerry's meeting with Derry despite predictions to the contrary. Hadn't people forecast a grim slog before their meeting in the previous year's semi-final? Instead we'd got the best game of 2023 as the two teams engaged in a thrilling shoot-out which Kerry edged in the closing stages. Maybe the boost of having beaten Mayo on penalties the week before would embolden Derry to go on the front foot like they had in the league final. Maybe being back in Croke Park would inspire Kerry to get the best from the array of attacking talent at their disposal. Maybe this was the day David Clifford would really turn it on. It could all happen.

Except it didn't. As John Cleese's frazzled headmaster says in the movie *Clockwise*, 'It's not the despair. I can take the despair. It's the hope I can't stand.'

The game was summed up by the Derry woman behind me who bellowed midway through the second half in a voice replete with irony, 'Come on, Derry, bore them into submission.' And the Donegal woman beside me gleefully reading out a message on her phone, 'Are you still stuck watching this atrocity?'

A certain amount of gallows humour had set in by this stage. It was the kind of thing you'd expect in a town where the streets had been flooded and the electricity cut off by a storm. The sheer awfulness of proceedings had united people in gleeful masochistic disbelief. This was a game to tell your grandchildren about. Preferably at Halloween.

It may well go down as a pivotal moment in football history, the day when everyone stopped pretending that the game would be alright as it was. Kerry and Derry made it clear that we couldn't go on like this. By doing so they did football a huge favour. The Football Review Committee under the chairmanship of Jim Gavin had been meeting to brainstorm ways of making the game more attractive. That quarter-final ensured that when the FRC presented its suggestions it would be pushing an open door. Declawing the report through the usual process of bureaucratic inertia wouldn't be an option. The FRC was not a talking shop, it was football's last hope. The All-Ireland final would be almost as bad but the die had been cast by then. Kerry and Derry provided football with its moment of clarity.

Things began misleadingly well with two sublime pieces of Clifford skill which suggested a tour de force might be in the pipeline. First came a beautiful solo point, a couple of dummies taking him past defenders before he tapped over the bar. Then he took an acrobatic mark under severe pressure and put that over too. At the other end Shane McGuigan, another of the game's artists, looked on fire early on and had kicked three points by half-time.

But as the game wore on, both Clifford and McGuigan were buried under the blanket of tedium which enveloped Croke Park like a pall of smoke from a burning rubbish dump. The passing was slow, the movement was lateral, the teams retreated into blanket defence at the slightest threat, and the game lost momentum as the players went about their job with all the *joie de vivre* of a chain gang repairing an Alabama road on a sweltering July afternoon. Describing it as dour was unfair to the word dour. Derry completely ran out of ideas and treated possession as an imposition rather than an opportunity. Kerry weren't much better but eventually ground out a five-point victory. This was Gaelic football as 'the ugly game', a sport which could give no pleasure to anyone except the more partisan supporters of the winning team.

The most galling thing was that the two teams had plenty of players, Clifford, McGuigan, Seán O'Shea, Paul Geaney, Conor Glass, Brendan Rogers, with the flair to produce something truly memorable. If they could produce a game like this, what hope did anyone else have? The supporters were in subdued mood leaving Croke Park. I think there was an awareness, or at least a hope, that we'd witnessed, if not the end of an era, at least the beginning of its end. After such football, what forgiveness? Heuston next morning resembled the main station in a city whose residents were flocking for the last trains ahead of an invading army. Though actually it was this army of teenagers and twentysomethings who'd been the invaders, swooping in that weekend to see not just Kansas City Chiefs tight end Travis Kelce's girlfriend but the Longitude Festival in Marlay Park, Shania Twain in Malahide Castle, Pride and The Saw Doctors in Fairview Park. It might have been the biggest weekend of communal fun in the city's history, the 1932 Eucharistic Congress and the papal visit having been more subdued affairs.

Now the jaded revellers were on their way back to Cork, Limerick, Galway, Castlebar and all points between, the glad rags replaced by hoodies, the make-up smudged, a general air of post-saturnalian exhaustion that made you yawn just to look at them. I remembered a similar feeling coming home from U2 at Croke Park in 1985, a concert much on my mind all these years later because this summer the stadium PA played 'Pride (In the Name of Love)' when one of the teams came out of the tunnel before the throw-in and again after half-time.

With the trains obviously booked out, the sensible thing was to get the bus. Except a nagging voice in my head said, *Maybe that's not why you want to get the bus. Maybe you're just using that as an excuse. Maybe you're back chickening out of getting the train again.* I told the voice that this obviously wasn't the case and that anyone could see getting this train would be the real madness. He wasn't impressed, so against my better judgement I bought a ticket with no seat number on it, decided to take my chances and joined in the charge which ensued when the platform number of the train came up.

By the time I got on, not only were all the seats taken but so were the prime sitting spots in the corridors. I managed to wedge myself next to the window but the crowds kept on coming so by the time we took off I was hemmed in by a couple of other guys and forced to assume the kind of restricted standing position an expert interrogator might have used to break down a prisoner. If I moved my arm, the guy next to me had to move his arm and the guy next to him had to move his arm. We tried not to do much moving. I thought of the relative comfort enjoyed by passengers in countries which, unencumbered by namby-pamby western concepts of health and safety, allow them to ride on the roof.

By Thurles I was able to stretch my arms and after Limerick Junction I got a seat across from three young Kerry women sharing two seats between them. They were talking, as myself and my brother Eoghan probably had been thirty-nine years previously, about the training they were doing and the matches they were going to play. Then they switched to the even more traditional Irish pastime of character assassination.

'You know what she said to me the other night? She said, "I run Rathmore now. I own this place."'

'She doesn't.'

'She said to me, "Oh, some day you'll realise all this small-town stuff you think is so important doesn't matter at all."'

'Don't mind her. She thinks she knows everything since she moved to Killarney.'

They were still shaking their heads at the arrogance of this urban sophisticate when they got off to change trains at Mallow.

18

Daughter Courage

I WATCHED THE CLARE–KILKENNY HURLING SEMI-final on the train from Cork to Dublin. When the final whistle blew on a Clare victory we were somewhere in Kildare. Cheers from Cork and Limerick fans alike rang through the carriage. Clare were many people's second-favourite team. They had a perennial underdog quality to them even when they were doing well.

Brian Lohan's team never got sufficient credit for pushing Limerick to the limit in the 2022 and 2023 Munster finals. Their subsequent semi-final defeats by Kilkenny had something to do with that. They'd cemented the idea that the Banner's lungs couldn't cope with the rarefied altitude of Croke Park. Now they'd disproved that one, winning by two points after being four down with ten minutes left, Shane O'Donnell switching to centre half-forward and orchestrating everything, Tony Kelly rounding things off with a magnificent long-range point.

Even after all that, Clare seemed to be flying under the radar. Their semi-final was just the support act for the following day's main event, perhaps the most hyped and most anticipated hurling semi-final of all time, the rematch between Cork and Limerick. The first semi had drawn 39,241, the second would fill Croke Park's 82,300 capacity. It would be the first ever full house hurling semi-final and had sucked up almost all the available oxygen of publicity. Cork–Limerick was Taylor Swift in the RDS. Clare–Kilkenny was Villagers at Trinity College. It couldn't have suited Lohan, O'Donnell and Kelly any better.

Cork and Limerick were too busy to notice but Clare were lurking in the shadows.

Why was I watching the first semi-final on the train rather than in Croke Park? Because making Croke Park on time would have involved taking the eight o'clock bus from Skibbereen. When I proposed doing so my daughter Isabel said, 'That doesn't surprise me,' in an unimpressed voice, and walked away from me.

This might not seem like much but by Isabel's standards it was going nuclear. She is a model of equanimity, someone with no morsel of malice or anger in her towards anyone. The only thing that normally upsets Isabel is cruelty, animal cruelty being particularly unbearable for her. But my semi-final schedule upset her and after a while I worked out why.

Between matches and family commitments at the other end of the country, I'd been missing the trips to Skibbereen Market with Isabel on Saturday which were part of our weekly ritual. Every week we buy a cookie from Anthony Boyle whose son Oisin is a member of the famous Skibbereen Rowing Club and has rowed for Ireland in the world junior championships. We buy plov, a combination of lamb and rice which is the national dish of Uzbekistan and which I'd happily eat every week of my life, from a man from the Crimea. We stroll along by the stalls run by the woman whose father was a well-known jazz musician in Dublin, another by the couple from Cork city who spent decades in east London where the husband won senior club medals in football. At these stalls and others like them I've bought the knick-knacks strewn through the house where I live, Russian dolls, porcelain cats, Toby jugs, Buddhist temple masks, wooden dolls from Nepal, Zambian coins, wooden zebras, panthers made of what I thought was ivory but am informed is jet, an assembly of the largely worthless but deeply loved. We buy felafel from a man from Israel who always has a fine soul music soundtrack playing in the background, bao from an English dude who used to be a deep-sea diving instructor, churros from a German who worked as a photographer with Agence France-Presse, duck eggs from two Castlehaven-supporting brothers with an invincible record in pub quizzes, books from a stall run by a friendly couple with cut-glass accents. We admire dogs of all shapes and sizes from chihuahuas to super-sized hounds, a preponderance of pooches who sometimes make the shoppers seem superfluous. On hectic summer days the place seems more a souk or bazaar than the slightly uptight designation of 'farmers' market'. Just as you never hear an Irish person call the Famine the 'Potato Famine', few people in Skibb call our market the 'farmers' market'.

This is our Saturday-morning routine and routine is very important to Isabel. Isabel is on the autism spectrum. She is eighteen and until two years ago we'd never had a conversation. When Isabel was younger she was diagnosed with cerebral palsy and we were told she'd need to use sticks to walk. We were also told she'd be in the smallest 5 per cent of the population.

Isabel is a talented artist who's won a prize in the Texaco Children's Art Competition. With every passing year she talks a bit more. Isabel never needed those sticks – they revised the palsy diagnosis and she'd walk the legs off anyone. Isabel is taller than her mother and quite a few other people. Isabel is the equivalent of one of those football teams which 'answered its critics'. Isabel is an overcomer.

Isabel knows the release year of any film she's ever watched, the studio which produced it and the other screen appearances of even the most minor actor involved. Isabel has a talent for one-liners which send the rest of us into stitches of laughter. Sometimes she laughs till her glasses fall off her face and the tears roll down her cheeks and we laugh along with her till

I slide off the couch and worry I might faint. We've spent a lot of time laughing together. Isabel sometimes seems to have a direct line to some source of distilled 100-per-cent-proof joy.

Isabel's life has its challenges but joy is its keynote. Her presence in my life has given me nothing but joy. If you'd asked me when I was ten I'd have told you my hero was Liam Brady. At twenty it was Lou Reed. At thirty it was Martin Luther King. At forty I'd probably have put a poncy puss on myself and quoted Bertolt Brecht's 'Unhappy is the land that needs heroes' line from *Mother Courage*. These days Isabel is my hero. She always will be from now on. Isabel is Daughter Courage.

While her sisters are in college, Isabel has started further education in Bantry. Taking the bus to and from there was a big step for her as regards independence. When I congratulated her she smiled and said, 'I'm not scared of buses,' with an emphasis on the *I'm*. Touché.

I'll leave it at that. The day will come when Isabel tells her full story in her own words. It'll be worth reading. But I knew on that Friday that I didn't want to miss any more Saturday markets with her. This book is after all less an exhaustive chronicle of the 2024 championship than a record of some things that moved me between April and July. Sitting out a couple of All-Ireland semis was unlikely to banjax the project. Even if it did, there are more important things in life than books or sport or work. From then till the end of the season I went to the market before taking the Saturday lunchtime train on which I watched Clare beat Kilkenny.

It's a venerable tradition with country people up for the match to get mass in Dublin. I remember my mother bringing me to the Pro Cathedral on the morning of the 1982 All-Ireland football semi-final which Galway lost by a point to an Offaly team for whom Brendan Lowry, father of the golfer Shane, scored a great goal. On the morning of this semi I also went the religious route but ended up taking a slight diversion. Christ Church Leeson Park, with its horizon-dominating spire, was just a few minutes from my B&B. It turned out to be hosting a Romanian Orthodox service. I hesitated in front of the door until a woman of considerable antiquity loitering in the porch, whose features could have appeared in the dictionary across from the word 'gnarled', said, 'You're very welcome,' and flashed me a smile whose gumminess was only exceeded by its friendliness.

You need to be tough for an Orthodox service. It lasts two hours and nobody sits. They could have that Sunday because, while a purposely designed Orthodox church has no seats at all, Christ Church had rows upon rows of them in the standard Irish configuration. Only a handful of old people used them and even then only for brief breathers.

The two hours should have dragged, especially since I didn't understand a word of the liturgy. On the rare occasions I do go to mass I'm one of those people thinking, *Forty-five minutes? What kind of sadism is this?* And I'm spending most of those forty-five minutes sitting down.

Instead I was fascinated. A lot goes on at an Orthodox service. Bells are rung at a great rate and big censers of incense waved flamboyantly towards the congregation. People dash forward to light candles and line up to kiss holy pictures. The altar is dominated by a screen on which a row of these starkly beautiful icons is displayed. All the while the priest is not speaking but singing the liturgy with austere elegance. There was a powerful sense of a mystery obscure to outsiders but available to those on its wavelength.

There were quite a few couples there who were around the same age, early twenties, that I'd been when I emigrated to London in 1988. My then girlfriend and myself would go to mass on Saturday evening in a church down the New Road which runs between Camberwell Green and the Oval. We probably wouldn't have gone if we were at home but there was something anchoring and consoling about the ritual in a strange city. The list of Irish names in the death notices almost made you feel like you were at home until the collection came round and, instead of a wooden bowl, you were handed a reinforced plastic contraption with a narrow security-minded slit at the top. It still seemed a place of respite and I suspected the young

Romanians, a lot further from home than we'd been, were getting the same kind of solace before facing into another week of grinding out a living in alien territory. Near the end the priest walked down the aisle and swung the censer in my direction. The odour of the incense felt other-worldly. The morning had been so incongruous with the city outside it almost came as a surprise to find Dublin still there when we came out.

Denigrating the capital is such an automatic culchie reflex I sometimes forget how beautiful Dublin can be. It was beautiful that Sunday afternoon as I sauntered along the canal bank. Two swans were out of the water and practically on the footpath preening themselves. They didn't pass a bit of heed when I sat next to them, took a photo and sent it to Isabel. It was time for Croke Park.

19

Sunday in Croke Park with Finbarr

LIMERICK HAD QUICKLY REGROUPED AFTER BEING caught on the hop in Páirc Uí Chaoimh. They'd looked as good as ever in a Munster final where their margin of victory was their biggest in the last five years, an ominous fact given that Limerick specialised in getting stronger as the season wore on and were a much more dangerous animal in Croke Park.

Meanwhile the electrifying hurling Cork had produced in Munster had been absent in stodgy victories over Offaly and Dublin. Limerick would be as firm favourites in Croke Park as they had been before the teams' earlier meeting.

Yet there was a feeling based more on intuition than logic that Cork were the one team with the potential to topple Limerick, their unpredictability and explosiveness giving them a puncher's chance. The feeling lent Croke Park its peculiar atmosphere that afternoon. The usual buzz of excitement was there but also the kind of calm-before-the-storm tension which prevails in the seconds before the gun sounds in an Olympic 100m final. We were waiting for the hurricane.

As I clambered my way up to perch in an eyrie near the top of the Cusack stand, the two-hour solidarity stand with the Romanian Orthodox didn't seem such a good idea after all. Two guys my own age took the seats beside me as throw-in approached. 'Finbarr,' said one of them, a rubicund sandy-haired guy built like a midfielder. 'Eamonn,' I replied, little imagining that we'd be locked in passionate embrace before the day was out.

The famous Cork confidence is sometimes subject to abrupt swings in the other direction. There was an unspoken fear that Limerick, stung by defeat in Munster, might retaliate by inflicting a repeat of the 2021 All-Ireland final humiliation. This was improbable because Cork had improved since then, but it was not impossible and that added to the tension. As throw-in approached, the appearance of absolute readiness in both teams made me think of the lines from *Henry V*, 'I see you stand like greyhounds in the slips / Straining upon the start'. The referee's whistle cried havoc, the dogs of war broke loose and battle was joined.

Cork came out of the traps like a favourite leading to the first bend at Shelbourne Park to go three points up after eight minutes. Limerick came after them like a dog gaining ground up the hill at the coursing in Clonmel and were level after ten. Cork went two up, Limerick pulled them back again. The game felt taut, as though any slackening by either side or moment of weakness by any player would be immediately punished. It had the fascination of a heavyweight title bout where the two big men had eschewed tactics and just set about pummelling each other as hard as possible from the opening bell.

At the midway point of the first half came the afternoon's first big breakthrough. Shane Barrett beat two defenders out on the left wing and passed to Brian Hayes who surged away from his man with the single-minded determination of an attacker who had nothing but goal on his mind. The angle wasn't easy but he buried the ball in the far corner. I jumped out of my seat as though propelled by an electric shock and roared. Finbarr was up too and we bellowed at each other like two kids in Halloween masks trying to frighten each other. I'm not even a Corkman but a combination of things, twenty-six years in the county, the exhilaration of watching this young team come back from the dead, the wild enthusiasm of the supporters on their first trip to Tipp, suddenly made a Cork victory enormously important to me. I felt that dumb visceral automatic identification I'd only previously felt for Sligo Rovers and Castlehaven. It was impossible not to get caught up in this game.

Surveying my seat up in the gods earlier on I'd thought being so far from the action would divorce me from the big-match atmosphere, that there'd be something bloodless about watching a game from such a height in this corner. In reality the game couldn't have felt more present to me if I'd been sitting below on the sideline. I'd actually been in almost the best place on the pitch to see Hayes take Barrett's pass and bear down on Nickie Quaid.

Some odd personal dynamics take hold during matches. You can find yourself making common cause with a fellow spectator, someone you've never met before, swapping oohs, aahs, meaningful looks, nods and winks during every significant moment of the game, looking for them to share the moments of maximum excitement. So it was with myself and Finbarr whose companion, a quiet bearded bloke with glasses, was the odd man out in this threesome. The communication doesn't even have to be verbal for you to share a match with someone in this way. Swapping tactical insights would take the heat out of things. Games like this one are felt rather than analysed. That's the joy of them.

Cork were running the legs off the Limerick defence again. That edge in pace was something even John Kiely and Paul Kinnerk's legendary tactical nous couldn't entirely negate. Three minutes later Cork cut through again and Alan Connolly set up Hayes for a second goal that should have put the outsiders seven points clear.

Referee Thomas Walsh disallowed it, ostensibly because Connolly had thrown rather than handpassed the ball. But TV replays confirmed there'd been nothing wrong with Connolly's pass. It was hard to escape the impression that the ref, seeing Cork dismantle the Limerick defence with such ease, had jumped to the conclusion that something must be up. The sight of the four-in-a-row All-Ireland champions going seven points down on his watch might have been an unnerving experience for a ref who, this moment apart, had an excellent game.

That decision started to look like a turning point as Limerick recovered and began to turn the screws on Cork. Winning all the aerial duels and the 50:50 contests, passing with precision and picking the Cork defence apart, they looked as good as they'd ever done. Their most gifted forward, Aaron Gillane, had been relatively quiet in the previous couple of games. Now he was suddenly his old unmarkable self, finding space, winning high and low ball and picking off points. The looks Finbarr and myself exchanged as Limerick went in at half-time were charged with foreboding. How could we have been so foolish as to yield to optimism against such opposition? It had taken Limerick until well into the second half in Cork to hit top gear and run the Rebels down. This time they'd done it with a half to spare. The mad optimism was leaching away again.

One row in front of us was a young girl dressed in Cork colours. Her parents were either side of her, dressed in Limerick colours. She cut a glum figure at the break.

'Don't worry,' Finbarr shouted down to her, 'you can travel home with us.'

Two rows in front of us was a shaven-headed Limerick fan in his thirties who looked like someone who'd either have trouble getting past bouncers or worked as one. As his team's comeback gathered steam he'd turn round and shake his fists triumphantly in the direction of the nearby Cork fans, like he'd just been acquitted in court and we were the prosecuting lawyers. The Cork fans were discussing the disallowed goal and imagining how different the game might have been had it been given. All the breaks needed to go your way against Limerick. They didn't give you a second chance to make a big impression.

It took Cork just a minute to equalise at the start of the second half. Limerick went one up within a minute. Cork were level a minute later. Then came a Cork blitz, six points in six minutes to Limerick's two. The Rebels were flying and the favourites were floundering but this was precisely the kind of situation where Limerick were most dangerous. In the forty-eighth minute Gearóid Hegarty, the Hammer of Cork, found himself in a position, twenty yards out and slightly to the right, from which he had arrowed several shots to the far corner in big games. He pulled the trigger and Patrick Collins made a brilliant save. But the ball fell right into the path of Gillane who seemed certain to flick it to the net. I could picture it nestling there already. Gillane closed in – and missed the ball. Cork defenders scrambled back and cleared it out to the right wing, where from just inside his own half Declan Dalton struck a monster point over the bar. There were twenty-two minutes remaining but I think in that moment Cork realised this was going to be their day. People would say there'd been a four-point swing, the missed goal followed by the point, but it felt more like a ten-point swing, the hinge on which the entire match turned. Dalton's shot was a pretty difficult one from long range but he seemed destined to land it. Hegarty's shot, Collins' save, Gillane's miss, Dalton's point, they were inextricably connected.

After the quarter minute encompassing them all, it became possible to imagine a world where Limerick weren't champions. Cork could see that and for the first time in five years Limerick could see it. Doubt was setting in.

Our shaven-headed friend two rows down raged against the dying of the light. Every free awarded against Limerick brought a roar, 'You fucking soft Cork cunts,' followed by a backwards glare to see if anyone had the bottle to disagree with this assessment. Finbarr took up the gauntlet. Every imprecation was met with an even louder shout of 'Come on the Rebels', after which he'd throw back his head and laugh with the whole-hearted delight of a child discovering some brilliant new game. You could nearly see the steam coming out of the Limerick man's ears. I noticed he had a buddy either side of him.

With Cork still seven points up eleven minutes from time it looked like their fans might be able to avoid the nerve-wracking tension of the Páirc Uí Chaoimh finale. But Limerick, who'd looked for most of the second half as if all the time on the road had finally caught up on them, summoned one last mighty effort. Nothing in their reign became them like the leaving of it. Gillane almost rescued them single-handed, his fire and fury in that final ten minutes evoking stories of Christy Ring throwing off his boots and socks to take on the Tipp defence in a 1951 Munster final which had been a paragon of excellence for an earlier generation. Ring's Cork fell short by two and so did Gillane's Limerick but there have been few games in which the defeated team lost so little caste.

Myself and Finbarr threw our arms open wide and fell upon each other. It was an emotional moment. I almost expected him to say 'Was it as good for you as it was for me?' but sometimes words just spoil the moment. We parted to find the Limerick skinhead looming over us.

'Just to say sorry, lads. I lose the run of myself at games. No hard feelings like.'

'No worries,' said Finbarr. 'Mind yourself.'

I suspected that had Limerick won, your man would have given it to us very hard. Finbarr knew that too and the Limerick man knew that we knew that but fair play to him, he'd come up the steps rather than slinking off. Unlike Mr This'll Be Remembered in Thurles, he'd done the right thing. Finbarr and myself swapped another bear hug and before we could get into the 'You say goodbye. No, you say goodbye' routine he headed off. Our brief encounter was over.

I stayed in the stand and let the unlikeliness of what had happened wash over me. Limerick had been so good for so long it wasn't just impossible to think of them being beaten, it was impossible to think of how it could even be done. Pat Ryan and his players had achieved hurling's equivalent of splitting the atom. The Cork fans were jubilant but they also seemed stunned by their team's effrontery. Just three years previously Limerick had stuck the biggest score in All-Ireland final history on Cork while easing off for most of the second half. Almost all the players from that game had played in this one. There'd been few turnarounds like this in GAA history.

As the Cork fans sought words to describe their feelings, music did it for them instead. Over the Croke Park PA came the Frank and Walters singing 'After All', that simplest, sweetest and most wonderful of indie love songs which sounded in that instant as though it had been created to specifically hymn the relationship between the Cork team and their fans.

The words were perfect but what really captured the spirit of the occasion was the bit at the end where Paul Linehan, as though from sheer joy at writing such a brilliant song, sings 'badadada badadabopbaba badadada badababopbaba' (or something along those lines, this is what I've always heard but it could be wrong). All over Croke Park Cork people were hopping up and down, punching the air and singing along as though these abstract syllables contained the very secrets of triumph and happiness itself. And when the song finished, the

PA operator, God bless him, played it again and got the very same reaction.

As I walked back towards town a couple of Cork lads were yelling, 'Goodbye five in a row,' over and over again. A tiny blonde wearing a Limerick jersey shouted after them, 'You try it and see how you get on.' The tears were pouring down her face and in that moment I was all on her side. I'd spent the last couple of years hoping Limerick would get beaten because I believed it's not good to have the same team winning repeatedly. Now they'd lost I realised how great it would have been to see them boldly go where no team had gone before and win five in a row. How often do you see history made? It would have been better if they'd lost next year instead. There's no pleasing some people.

Perhaps the biggest tribute to Limerick's stature was that even though there were two All-Ireland finals remaining, one of which would be an even better match, this semi-final would still seem like the biggest match of the year when the championships ended. Limerick were such an overpowering force, nothing could exceed the impact of seeing them dethroned. This had happened before. Mayo's ambush of the six-in-a-row Dubs in the semi-final seemed a more significant part of the 2021 football season than the scrappy final they lost to Tyrone. The semi-finals of 2011 and 2014 which Dublin and Donegal split between them dwarfed the deciders of those years.

As the Cork fans surfed through the inner-city streets on a wave of euphoria it was easy to forget that the final still lay ahead. Easy to forget too that, after all the fireworks, this semi-final had ended up mirroring their earlier win over Limerick. The provincial form had held up, with two points the margin on both occasions. It was also the margin by which Clare had beaten Cork in the Munster championship.

But who was thinking of such things after such a victory?

20

Desperadoes Chatting on a Train

A BIG, BURLY, BEARDED GUY PACED UP AND DOWN the Dublin to Cork train like an unhappy polar bear measuring his enclosure. He peered out the door a couple of times, looking so jumpy I wondered if he might suffer from the same problem as myself. He calmed down when his friend arrived. The pair of them sat beside each other on the seat in front of mine.

A pale, small, well-turned out man in his forties took the seat opposite them. The train had just moved out of Heuston when they asked where he was going. He muttered an inaudible answer.

'We're going to Portlaoise. Portlaoise is a shit hole. Abbeyleix is good, a lot going on there, good crack. Mountmellick is better than Portlaoise. Portlaoise is a shit hole.'

Or shih hole to be more precise. There was a pent-up energy about the two lads, who looked in their twenties and wore identical leather jackets, a sense of impatience with the constraints of the seat and the coming boredom of the journey.

'What do you work at yourself?'

'I'm a barrister.'

'Oh. He's just after getting out of prison.'

The unmistakable joy in the bearded lad's voice suggested he'd just encountered a fellow countryman on a lonely day in a foreign land. His friend, who looked a bit like the actor Timothée Chalamet, sat up stock straight as though spring-operated and practically pricked up his ears in delight at the coincidence of meeting someone in the same line of work.

'Mountjoy is a tough place to be in at the moment. There's lads sleeping on the floor with overcrowding,' said the newly released prisoner.

'A tough place,' agreed his friend. 'But the thing to do is try and get a job in the kitchens. You're treated better then, you have more freedom.'

'Were you busy today? Were you in the Four Courts or the CCJ?'

The barrister said he'd been in the Criminal Courts of Justice.

His companions listed off a litany of barristers and solicitors and asked if he knew them.

'X is our solicitor. He's brilliant, a very educated man. He sticks up for you.'

He didn't say X obviously but we might as well be on the safe side, though anyone would be proud to receive the kind of reference they provided.

'Like, the last time I got eight months. I could easily have got two or three years.'

'Do you mind me asking,' said the barrister politely, 'what you were up for?'

'Robbery,' said Chalamet.

'I'm out on bail for a rake of offences at the moment,' interjected his friend.

'It's hard cause when you're doing time, your woman and child are doing time too. They're going through the hardship as well. His woman left him in July.'

'But I see the kids twice a week, they sleep over and that. I went to rehab, it cost me nineteen thousand euros. I'm clean ten weeks. I'm trying to turn my life around.'

'Me too, I'm going out with a fine-looking woman.'

'She is a fine-looking woman. This time I'll turn it round.'

'You should do it,' said the barrister kindly. 'You can turn your life round in six months.'

'Six weeks,' said the bearded fella.

'Six days,' chipped in Chalamet.

'Are you signing on?'

'Three times a week at the garda station and a curfew at eight o'clock. I can look out my front door and that's it. I have to make sure I'm home.'

The barrister thought this sounded very restrictive and wondered if it might be better to get an ankle bracelet with an electronic tag fitted instead.

'If you saw one of them, an alarm goes off.'

'The one thing we have going for us is our families. They always stick by us. A lot of them turn up to back us in court.'

'I don't like guards. I did some of the things I'm up for but they had nothing on me on the others. I don't like them. I think a lot of guards is fellas that was bullied at school and they become guards to be bullies themselves.'

'You must have some guards that you get on with.'

'Ah we do. A lot of them are OK,' said Chalamet, nodding his head and shooting the barrister a complicitous glance to establish their mutual status as the reasonable men in this conversation.

'Have you thought of getting a job?'

'I was in building one time. What do you think of personal injuries? It can be a lot of money for a small thing.'

The trolley was passing through the carriage as we pulled into Portlaoise and the two lads ordered a can of Coke apiece. The barrister interceded to pay for it and Chalamet spent so much time saying thanks he almost missed his stop.

It had been deadly quiet in the carriage since the conversation began. Not a tense silence but that of an audience paying rapt attention. A middle-aged man broke it.

'Every day is a school day.'

'You didn't expect to be giving out free advice,' another middle-aged man said to the barrister. There was an invitation to betrayal in those words. The barrister could say something like, 'You see the kind of people I have to deal with,' and everyone could smile and nod and feel superior. Instead he said, 'I've heard a lot worse,' in a manner which let you know this would be his last word on the matter. He was protecting lawyer/client privilege. I was glad he'd taken that tack. Perhaps most of my fellow passengers were too and allowed themselves to dream that the Laois desperadoes might really manage to turn their lives around this time. There had been an odd innocence about the way they talked. They weren't boasting or apologising for their deeds, just offering them up to make friendly conversation and shorten the journey.

That was on the Monday after the football semi-final between Galway and Donegal. On the Saturday the trip to the market with Isabel meant I'd watched another semi on the train. Kerry were playing Armagh and, when I got off at Heuston, seemed en route to the same kind of clinical victory they'd ground out against Derry. They were five up with twenty minutes left and apparently in total control.

As I was getting my Luas ticket from the machine, Armagh scored a weird goal. Kerry keeper Shane Ryan who was normally flawless from kick-outs botched one and Armagh got possession. Rian O'Neill shot from a range where he'd normally score but the shot fell well short. Ryan who was normally very good under the high ball spilled this one and Barry McCambridge, the Armagh corner-back, punched it into the net on the bounce.

The strange nature of the score might have helped to unsettle Kerry. Or it could have been, like Dublin against Galway, they'd become so used to cruising mode that they'd forgotten the location of the extra gears. By the time I got to the hotel Armagh had forced the game into extra-time. They were the better team and I watched them come through by two points while walking down Parnell Street to see an Indian film, *Kalki 2898 AD*, in Cineworld.

The movie featured an evil 200-year-old king, a reincarnated god with a magic jewel in his forehead, a floating pyramid and a serum which confers superhuman powers. None of these things seemed more unlikely than Armagh's victory. Or than David Clifford's failure to make an impact on the match. The big game we'd waited for him to produce all year had never arrived. He seemed worn down by what football had become and he wasn't alone. The All-Star team at the end of the season would contain none of the game's acknowledged star forwards. All six attackers would be first-time selections and two of them had largely played as auxiliary midfielders. It was that kind of year.

Kalki 2898 was great, by the way. Like a cross between

Star Wars, *Mad Max* and *The Mahabharata*. And the Cork–Limerick semi-final because it never let up for a second. *Kalki* was the latest in a line of Indian blockbuster epics which broke box office records at home and did serious business abroad too. They weren't Bollywood but Tollywood, made by the Telugu language film industry based in the city of Hyderabad. Surrounded by exhilarated South Indians in Cineworld, I might have been watching the film over there. Watching Indian movies seemed more like going to a match than like the more subdued, normal cinema experience. There was even a half-time, a break during which fifteen minutes counted down backwards on the screen like the timer on a bomb in a thriller while the crowd replenished themselves with stock from the shop and returned for the second half, primed to throw themselves back into the action. It seemed a pretty unbeatable way to watch movies.

The streets of Dublin were full of memories that Sunday morning. O'Connell Street is an uncanny valley at that time, the noise of the night before dying away between the buildings while the footpaths are ceded to the tourists, the energetic, the anxious and the lonely. On mornings like this writing the first book I'd wake up with no way to hold my head that didn't hurt and venture shakily out accompanied by the rest of the lyrics from 'Sunday Morning Coming Down'. The hangovers had gone but the lonesome sound of the song stayed with me.

I ducked into a café on Bachelors Walk called Murphy's Bistro and run by Turkish people. Did that confuse the Yanks who were my fellow customers? I ate a gorgeous mix of eggs, tomatoes, chillies and peppers called menemen. A sense of childish joy washed over me as I dipped bread into the egg's gooey innards. Few things are more fun than dashing bread across a plate. It brings you back, like running through puddles. The Turkish coffee was a Niall Cahalane of coffee – it wasn't taking any nonsense from anyone.

Later I walked around Rathmines where I'd lived when I first came to the city, in a tiny bedsit on Grove Park with a monkey puzzle tree outside the window, a trip switch in the hall and a drunken civil servant down the landing who'd arrive at the door in the early hours bearing bottles of Guinness and reminisce about his Offaly childhood. I'd marvelled at the urban sophistication of the city's only twenty-four-hour shop and its first Abrakebabra. After coming back from England I moved to Effra Road and tramped down to the Swan Centre to feed a stream of coins into the upstairs phones in a largely unavailing search for freelance work.

Down the end of the main drag on a leafy street where Rathmines starts petering into Rathgar I sat out under the awning of Deli 613, the first kosher restaurant to open in Dublin for half a century, and ate a delicious salt beef sandwich. As I ordered, a Dublin family, the father wearing a kippa, arrived for a function and the rabbi came out to greet them. A few hundred yards away was a Palestinian restaurant, Bethlehem, where I got a takeaway that night. Arabic music played in the back-ground and there was a warmth about the place which made me sorry to leave it. As I took away my musakhan chicken the effusively friendly host told me, 'You'll like this, you're going to like this so much that you'll want to come back here and have a meal with your whole family.' He was right.

21

Johnno's Farewell

JOHN O'MAHONY HAD DIED EIGHT DAYS BEFORE the Galway–Donegal football semi-final at the age of seventy-one. He was probably the most under-rated of all great football managers. The Galway All-Ireland win in 1998 was one of those rare occasions when a team comes from nowhere to go all the way. Their easy win over Meath three years later was just as unexpected.

I remembered him less as a great manager than as someone who, with his wife Geraldine, had been very kind to me as a teenage trainee reporter on the *Roscommon Herald* charged with collecting local notes from him in Ballaghaderreen. I was gauche, nervous, cripplingly shy and seriously wondering whether a job involving so much personal interaction was right for me. The cups of tea and chat they'd offered had worked wonders for my confidence. They'd thrown me a lifebelt. Small acts of kindness go a very long way. Longer than those responsible would ever suspect.

He'd once told me that he'd never been more relaxed than on the morning of the 2001 final. He knew that he and the team had done all the work they'd planned to do and that no matter what was thrown at them they couldn't be better prepared. It was a fantastic feeling, he said, and smiled at the memory of it.

That moment has stuck with me. Before every single exam my daughters have sat, from Junior Cert to Leaving Cert to university, I tell them about how John O'Mahony felt on the morning of the 2001 final and that they should feel the same way. It's a kind of family talisman. Every time my daughters do an exam they have John O'Mahony with them. That's my tribute to the man.

Croke Park's tribute before the game was a montage of his great years, with 'To Win Just Once' by The Saw Doctors playing behind it. If grown men weren't crying, they were certainly doing a lot of gulping and looking at their feet.

The crowd was a big one, almost 12,000 up on Armagh–Kerry and almost 25,000 on the Sunday football semi-final the previous year. Galway generally lagged far behind Mayo support-wise, they'd had less than half as many fans at their home quarter-final, but the win over Dublin had brought them out. Yet the noise and the energy largely came from the

Donegal fans. The force was with them. With Galway and Armagh having cleared Dublin and Kerry out of the way they were poised to strike, like an athlete who rounds the last bend and sees a gap open up in front of them. Jimmy was only two winning matches away from an even bigger miracle than his first one.

The problem was that while Galway were not a fun team to watch, they were even less fun to play against. They were big and physical enough to win plenty of possession and hang on to it for a long time. Donegal also employed a possession game but Galway's build-up was glacial and tended to turn their matches into wars of attrition. They were grinders who backed their ability to grind teams down. The high-speed counter-attacks and sudden injections of pace which made Donegal so irresistible never materialised. Most telling of all was the virtual anonymity of Peadar Mogan and Ryan McHugh.

Former Galway manager Kevin Walsh had been asked the previous week if he thought Galway would assign man-markers to Mogan and McHugh. He seemed amused by the idea. Galway, he said, would simply put up a line of defenders fifty-five yards out and make sure Mogan and McHugh ran into traffic when they got the ball. As coach of the Cork team which had beaten Donegal his words carried some weight.

His prediction came true: Galway played a narrow defence, gummed up the middle and shepherded Donegal's flyers out to the harmless territory of the wings. It was canny stuff by Pádraic Joyce and showed that in this era of football there was no one whose influence couldn't be negated by sheer weight of numbers. Mogan and McHugh had scored a combined 1–12 in their previous two games. Galway didn't just hold them scoreless, they limited them to a combined total of one shot.

Things didn't go entirely to plan for Galway either. The feeling was that they'd need big games from Shane Walsh and Damien Comer. Neither scored and both looked to be carrying injuries. Galway found it difficult to bring their most potent weapons into play. That plodding build-up must have been an inside forward's nightmare. It would have driven Joyce, a full-forward who thrived on quick ball, mad during his playing days.

This was John Maher weather instead. Maher was like Shane Walsh's doppelganger from an alternative universe, the antithesis of what people thought of as a 'lovely footballer'. Players like Maher are the self-made men of football. With no inheritance of natural skill or speed they have to work for everything they get. There's something heart-warming about watching them in action. Maher reminded me of Colm McManamon who'd played for Mayo in the nineties. The awkwardness of McManamon's style drew occasional derision but he was something of a folk hero, a football equivalent to those Stakhanovite labour heroes in communist states lauded for record-breaking feats down the mines or in the shipyard. His performances showed how far hard work could take you.

Maher was the same. In his first game for Galway he'd been taken off at half-time and didn't get called up again for a year. Since then he'd bobbed in and out of the team in the way players do when managers know they're probably the best option at the moment but wish they had a better one.

Now he'd established himself in the team. He still seemed a little one-paced, his face always looked like playing the game was agony but no one had done more to get Galway this far. Ostensibly a wing-forward, he got up and down the field all day. If a Galway player was under pressure in defence and needed someone to pass to, up popped Maher. If they needed to turn defence into attack, Maher was there to provide the link. If an attack was stalling and needed someone to break a tackle to keep the momentum going, you know who did the needful. He didn't do anything particularly fancy with the ball but he didn't give it away. He shirked no challenge. He was, to use an old phrase, a hoor for hard work and he was all over this semi-final. On a grinding team, Maher was the grindmeister supreme.

It was a weekend for weird goals. The teams were level in the twenty-fifth minute when Paul Conroy shot for a point from forty-five yards. Conroy, like Rian O'Neill, was one of the best in the game from long range but this was one of his poorer efforts. It dropped well short, bounced and flew into the net past Shaun Patton who'd been distracted by an inrushing Matthew Tierney.

The goal was jammier than a packet of Jacob's Mikados. Like Armagh's goal against Kerry it raised the possibility that the best key for unlocking blanket defences might be a poor kick. Kerry's goal had also originated from a point attempt that was going wide being knocked back into play. As if to underline how flukey his goal was, when Conroy got a similar chance just before half-time he put it over the bar.

A score like that could have been a devastating blow for Donegal but they fought back to draw level at half-time. This was largely due to three lovely points from Michael Langan, a player just a couple of letters away from being an example of nominative determinism. His name was Langan and his style was languid. At his best he looked like he had an infinity of time to spare on the ball. This was one of his very best days as he went placidly amid the noise and haste to arrow three shots over the bar and keep Donegal in touch.

Level when the second half began, they were level again fifteen minutes into it. It was tense, and between the fiftieth and sixtieth minutes tension got the better of both teams. They were stuck in the desert on a horse with no name as the game degenerated into a stalemate and no one scored for eleven minutes. You had a hunch that whoever found their way out of this impasse first would prevail in a match which both teams seemed more concerned about not losing than winning.

Cometh the hour, cometh the Mahcr, who barrelled forward and fisted over as two defenders converged upon him, one of them delivering a dunt which tumbled the big man as the ball bisected the posts. The two players who did the spadework, Liam Silke and Dylan McHugh, had done to Donegal what Mogan and Ryan McHugh normally did for them. The defenders split four points between them, just one less than the Galway attack managed from play.

Two minutes later the teams were level for the tenth time, Langan bombing over another beautiful point. It was an individual tour de force fated to be largely forgotten. He'd kept Donegal in the game single-handed, or maybe double-handed because Oisín Gallen had chipped in with three fine points from play. The young full-forward wasn't quite the new Michael Murphy but he could be mentioned in the same sentence without fear of ridicule.

Fans of both persuasions looked like children watching *Doctor Who*, unable to tear their eyes away but nervous about the next twist in the plot. There were six minutes left and the teams were level when Donegal won a free. The Galway fans near me looked sick. Gallen stepped up to take it. It wasn't an easy free but would have been classed as tricky rather than difficult. He'd landed tougher shots with defenders hanging out of him. But he pulled this one wide. There could have been no better illustration of the effects of pressure and it seemed to knock the stuffing out of Donegal, the way a missed putt in the closing holes of a major costs a player more than one extra stroke.

Galway took the lead a minute later and stretched it out to two entering injury-time, Silke fisting over after the indefatigable Maher had done the donkey work. In the end it probably came down to the fact that Galway had won an All-Ireland semi-final two years ago and knew what it took to win big games in Croke Park. Suddenly you remembered how far McGuinness had brought Donegal this year and what unaccustomed territory this was for his players. When Langan sent a shot a mile wide at the start of injury-time, you knew it was curtains for them.

It was a tough one to lose but the disappointment of the Donegal fans was that of game show contestants who've won a lot of money but missed out on the grand prize. They'd been in bonus territory. McGuinness had brought them so far so quickly, there'd be an exciting winter ahead thinking of next year's possibilities. It got even more exciting when Michael Murphy declared he'd come out of retirement next season, the equivalent for full-back lines everywhere of seeing Glenn Close rise out of the bath in *Fatal Attraction*.

Galway's victory was the most fitting denouement. On the day of that 2001 All-Ireland final against Meath when John

O'Mahony woke up knowing he'd got everything right, Pádraic Joyce gave one of the great individual displays in football history. He'd kicked five points from play against Darren Fay, a full-back regarded as almost invincible, and the Connacht champions overwhelmed the hot favourites. Now Joyce was on the sideline. Would he also get everything right on the big day? We'd find out in a fortnight.

22

The Final Countdown

MY ALL-IRELAND HURLING FINAL DAY HAD A Russian feeling. Sunday morning was like Dostoyevsky, Sunday afternoon was like Chekhov and the game was like Tolstoy.

I was staying in Rathmines again, not from nostalgia but because you take what you get on All-Ireland final weekend. The hotel breakfast room was a sea of Cork jerseys. It was like being back on the train to Thurles but with less noise. 'That's the eating done for the day,' said one man as he laid down his knife and fork.

Dostoyevsky's haunted protagonists spend a lot of time searching for the 'Russian soul'. They never looked for it in Harold's Cross. The St Peter and St Paul Church had been built as a Protestant church in the nineteenth century and consecrated as a Russian Orthodox church in 2003. It was near where I'd watched Sligo Rovers play St Pat's at the old Harold's Cross greyhound stadium and where my father had gone up in smoke at the Mount Jerome Crematorium. I hadn't great memories of either occasion.

I'd been genuinely moved by the Romanian Orthodox service two weeks previously. Irreligious though I am, it had stuck with me and I wanted to experience something similar. The Russian service was more powerful still because it took place in a church expressly given over to the purpose. The complete absence of pews made the congregation seem like owners rather than tenants of the premises. It gave the space a sense of expansiveness you didn't usually get in an Irish parish church. Watching women come in, collect scarves and tie them around their heads, I remembered my grandmother and the other older women with their heads covered in the same way at mass in Spiddal.

My grandparents on my mother's side had been religious in the way everyone of their generation had. Early in his married life my grandfather went drinking with a friend. As he returned to the house, a picture of the Virgin Mary fell down off the wall and its glass shattered. He'd taken this as a sign and never drank again. His daughter Bríd became a nun. My mother remembered travelling up to Dublin with my grandfather to spend a few minutes talking to her through a grille at a Convent of Mercy. She remembers too my grandfather's quiet upset on the way home. When Bríd left the convent, my grandmother would wait behind after mass to avoid the cruel comments she felt might be aimed at her on the way home.

Yet their faith was never shaken. I remember as a small child being awoken by a strange rumbling sound in their house and emerging from the bedroom in my pyjamas to find the household on its knees saying the rosary in Irish before turning in for the night. It was impossible, my father used to say, for someone of my generation to realise the ubiquity of religion in everyday life for someone of his generation. The traces of it that remained in my childhood seem very strange to my children.

Religion was the element in which my grandparents' generation moved, like fish in water. It was just there, monolithic and implacable. When I think of its effect on them, I think of what Winston Churchill said about whiskey, that he'd got more out of it than it had got out of him but it had been a close-run thing. I don't know. There's no way for me to know. But while the Harold's Cross service was strange on one level, the seriousness of its ceremony and the strength of its conviction was also oddly familiar. It brought me back.

I'd mentally practised the Orthodox sign of the cross on the way up in the hope of not looking too much of a stranger. Some chance. The Orthodox service is very kinetic by comparison to the Catholic one. In addition to the lighting of candles and venerating of icons, people are constantly blessing themselves, sometimes sweeping their hand towards the floor as they do so, and dropping to their knees. One look at the floor made me realise that if I dropped to my creaky knees without assistance, I'd be stuck there for the rest of the morning. The Russians of all ages knelt and I stood. They're a hardy bunch.

All the while, the priest sang the liturgy. At one stage the congregation joined in and sang along with him for several minutes. It was one of the most beautifully lyrical things I'd ever heard, the voices melding perfectly in chorus within the walls of this building in this ordinary suburb. It was the sound of holy minimalism, the only modern classical music with popular appeal thanks to Orthodox composers like Arvo Pärt and John Tavener, being sung not by a choir but by people who'd be back at work the following morning, 'The Protecting Veil' live, round the corner from the defunct dog track. It was one of those moments when music made you feel like you always hope it will when you start listening. Logic alone didn't put you in that space. There was something else and perhaps the search for it would always draw people into the churches, the mosques, the synagogues, the temples, the gospel halls and the gurdwaras.

After the service ended people queued up at the back of the church to buy religious accoutrements. I picked up a small wooden icon of the Virgin Mary as a present for my mother and, as I went to pay for it, realised there was no card machine and I didn't have enough cash. The woman in charge realised the situation, smiled at me and gestured that it would be OK.

Next morning I went back and bought an icon case upholstered in red velvet which opens out to reveal God the Father on the right and Mary with the infant Jesus on the left. They've looked down on me from the bookshelves as I've written every word of this book. Occasionally I imagine Russian God whispering, 'He's no Dostoyevsky, I'll tell you that.'

The Luas had just pulled out of Beechwood station when a young lad in a Cork jersey fainted. He'd gone the colour of the title character from *Corpse Bride* by Tim Burton. Momentary panic ensued in the packed carriage.

'Is there a doctor? Is there a doctor?'

There was, a guy in his thirties with a Cork accent who told us to give the lad space, checked his pulse and announced he'd be OK. At Ranelagh station people jumped out of the carriage and ran along the platform to inform the driver he'd have to stop the tram till an ambulance got here.

'No, no,' said the young lad in what would have been a shout if he hadn't been so weak, 'I'll be alright.'

The doctor concurred, so other people jumped out to tell the driver the first instruction had been cancelled. Normal service was resumed but the doctor said it was still a good idea to give the young lad space and let him lie down on the floor. A woman in her thirties manned the nearest door with the ferocity of an underfed Alsatian guarding a scrapyard and forbade anyone to enter or exit by it. This worked grand and the patient picked up a bit of strength as we approached the city centre. As we neared the first O'Connell Street stop, an American, nearer thirty than twenty stone and sweating profusely, made his way down the carriage and towards the door.

'You can't go out here.'

'Why not?'

'He's not well. Go down and get out another door.'

The American looked stunned. He turned away, retreated a few steps and then turned back, shouting, 'You gotta let me out, you gotta let me out, you just gotta let me out.'

The look on his face suggested he thought we were about to rob or maybe eat him. Before the gatekeeper could block him he produced a shockingly nimble leap for a huge dude which carried him over the fainting Cork man and into the street just before the doors closed.

We wished the young lad well as he got off at the other end of O'Connell Street. 'I hope you're not a bad omen,' someone said. They hoped in vain.

A kid selling bottles of water opposite Fitzgibbon Court flats was there as I walked to the ground. His sister was doing cartwheels beside him.

I really like Anton Chekhov. The short stories are great but I retain a special *grá* for the plays. *The Cherry Orchard* is the best of the lot. There's something almost unbearably poignant about aristocrats in their country house knowing their way of life is doomed and unable to do anything about it. Especially with our knowledge of how cruel their fate is going to be after the revolution we know is coming down the pipeline.

That seems weird considering that, like most of us, I'm descended from the peasant class liberated by the decline and fall of the aristocracy all over Europe. So are most people who enjoy *Downton Abbey*. Such sagas are made bearable by our knowledge that the system they portray is on its last legs. A pinch of *schadenfreude* helps them go down easier. Chekhov had mixed feelings himself. As the grandson of a serf he was one of us rather than one of them.

I loved those plays but never thought I'd end up like one of the characters. Yet there seemed something very Chekhovian about the scenario as I entered the press box that afternoon. The assembled journalists were the last relics of a world as surely doomed as the one in which Madame Ranevskaya had lived. No one would ever have mistaken us for aristocrats but the life we'd known was also being swept away by the tide of history and there was nothing we could do about it either.

Social media had moved fast and broken the newspaper industry, hoovering up ads and providing news for free online. The combined loss of advertising and circulation revenue was crippling. Local papers bit the dust, national papers cut jobs and started focusing on the website rather than the print edition. You could smell the blood in the water. Everything that once seemed solid was melting into air.

Papers were doomed by the advent of social media in the same way that the horse-drawn coach industry was by the arrival of the motor car. They hit the buffers everywhere in the western world. The most brilliant management possible couldn't have saved them in their old form. Within a decade all Irish newspapers will probably have become websites. Last month the *Evening Standard* moved from daily to weekly and renamed itself the *London Standard*. Maybe our national papers will make that stop on the way or maybe we'll just go straight to online only. What do I know? I'm just a journalist.

Being resigned to the fate of the newspaper industry doesn't mean I'm not sad about it. As Ogden Nash wrote, 'The old men know when an old man dies.' Looking at the guys milling around the room downstairs where you get some grub and a cup of tea before ascending to the box proper, I felt a huge surge of affection. It surprised me and would have surprised them even more. There were journalists there I'd never agreed with on anything and the feeling was mutual. But now we were all in the same boat and it was sinking.

I felt especially for those my own age and older. This was in most cases the only job they'd known. They'd begun like myself standing on the side of pitches doing obscure club matches for local papers and worked their way up. They were good at their job in ways perhaps only a fellow professional properly appreciated.

They could turn around a thousand-word match report five minutes after the final whistle by writing it as the game went along yet make it read as though it had been composed in one coherent sweep. That was a skill which took years of practice to pick up and there were guys there who could do it standing on their head. They got their facts right, they knew what was happening, they could predict team selections, they spotted changes of position immediately, they could find something of interest in the most prosaic quote or the least remarkable team announcement. They were pros.

Few things make us feel happier, says the *Washington Post* literary critic Michael Dirda, than the exercise of professional competence. Watching it being done can make you feel pretty good too.

It was years since I'd been in a press box. It's much less enjoyable to watch a game there than from the stands or the terraces because, after all, it's a workplace. A famous American book about the great sportswriters of the twenties and thirties is called *No Cheering in the Press Box*. That rule still holds. Being back in the press box changed me from the Cork fan I'd been in the semi-final back into a journalist. Muscle memory clicked in and professional detachment descended upon me. It didn't matter. The 2024 All-Ireland hurling final required no partisan allegiance to make it thrilling. Someone who'd never seen a game in their life would have realised something extraordinary was unfolding in front of them.

23

The Greatest Game

THE 2024 ALL-IRELAND HURLING FINAL WAS AN EPIC containing so many twists and turns it seemed to go on for much longer than the hour-and-a-half-plus the teams spent on the field. This was the *War and Peace* of hurling finals.

The start of the game seemed impossibly distant by the time the final whistle blew. It was scarcely believable that in the twelfth minute I'd been hoping that Clare might manage to hang on so the match wasn't over as a contest by half-time. That was after Robert Downey had fielded Eibhear Quilligan's puck-out just inside his own half and powered into Clare territory with Peter Duggan trying vainly to catch him. As Downey kept going you presumed he'd fire a shot over the bar. The Clare backs seemed to presume the same. Forty yards out, thirty yards out and the presumption had now become a hope from the Banner's point of view. Downey still hadn't been challenged when he was twenty yards out, whereupon he flicked the ball up and volleyed it into the net. It was a brilliant run and an even better finish but a foreign spectator might have wondered if some rule of hurling prevented anyone other than Duggan challenging the Cork player.

Downey and his team-mates had taken up where they'd left off against Limerick and Clare seemed to have no answer. Cork were running away from them like wild horses over the hills. By the fourteenth minute they were seven points up and streets ahead of Clare in every part of the field.

It was Shane O'Donnell time. He probably knew another couple of Cork scores might put the game beyond Clare's reach and that a drastic intervention was essential. The ball which came his way in the seventeenth minute, a long, high David McInerney delivery that left him with a 50:50 contest against the taller Ciarán Joyce near the left sideline, wasn't ideal but O'Donnell specialised in making the most of things. He was the hurling alchemist who turned base metal into gold. O'Donnell broke the ball down, extricated himself from Joyce's grapple, snapped up the sliotar, eluded another attempted Joyce hold and found Peter Duggan. Duggan cut inside and, finding his way barred, returned the ball to O'Donnell who'd kept running and was a step ahead of Joyce. He sidestepped the challenge of Eoin Downey, dived through the tackle of Robert Downey and while falling got away a handpass to Aidan McCarthy who stuck the ball in the net.

In a game overflowing with sublime moments of skill, O'Donnell's intervention was something very different. His swerving, ducking, diving, sniping progress might have been that of a scrum-half seeking an opening in the opposition 22. After flicking the ball into his hand on the wing he never put it on the hurl again. The run had less to do with skill than will and O'Donnell's tenacious determination to unlock the Cork defence by any means necessary because the Banner were in bad need of a boost.

He added two more points in the next four minutes to leave Clare just two behind. There was a long way to go and many more things would happen but the run by O'Donnell was the most important moment of the day. Up to that Cork had been playing as though the final was an extension of the semi-final. The confidence gained by beating Limerick was practically dripping off them. The goal turned the game back into a contest in its own right, a contest against a team which had already beaten them this year. They'd never be quite the same again. Neither would Clare. O'Donnell's run was their El-Alamein moment. Before it they never looked winning, after it they never looked like losing.

The teams were level at half-time and five minutes after the break Mark Rodgers scored probably the most under-rated goal in All-Ireland final history. He burst on to a loose ball just inside the Cork half, outpaced one defender, sidestepped another and with a third closing on him sent a rocket past Collins. It would have been the outstanding moment in many finals, destined to be pored over again and again, but so much happened in this match it almost got lost. Rodgers' individual performance would have won him man-of-the-match awards in other finals. But he was about to get seriously outshone.

When Tim O'Mahony levelled things again in the forty-seventh minute I heard someone shout that Clare should take Tony Kelly off. With everyone else rising to the pitch of this great final, Kelly was the odd man out. He was enduring another inexplicable afternoon when he seemed to be on the outside looking in. His marker O'Mahony was having the game of his life and had hit three fine points.

That Clare were leading an All-Ireland final with Kelly anonymous showed how far they'd come but they still needed him to awaken if they were to win it. Redemption was just seven seconds away.

50 minutes 50 seconds: Kelly has one Cork defender breathing down his neck and another standing in his way as he takes a pass from David Fitzgerald thirty-five yards out.

50:51: He's accelerated away from the first defender and swerved to the right past the second. A third comes in to block his path.

50:52: He's veered past that defender and there are now five Cork backs in a horizontal line behind him trying to get back.

50:53: Kelly is cutting in towards goal and a last covering defender comes across to make a tackle.

50:54: As one of the chasing pack closes on him, Kelly flicks the ball over the head of the final defender.

50:55: He darts forward and, as two defenders move within arm's reach of him, controls the ball with one flick of the hurl and sweeps it past the advancing Collins with another.

50:56: The ball is in the net and Kelly, sent flying by a collision with Collins, still manages to spread his arms wide in a gesture of celebration.

It was, taking the occasion and the state of play into account, probably the greatest goal ever scored in Croke Park. It's hurling's equivalent of Maradona's second goal against England (hurling's equivalent of his first would arrive before the afternoon was out). Breaking it down into its constituent parts does it an injustice because it was all about speed, fluidity and the ability to do things instinctively. This kind of skill exists at the level of instinct rather than thought because hurling at its peak is, like jazz, an improvised art. Kelly's goal is like a perfect moment in a solo which can be notated but could not be predicted and cannot be repeated. It's a moment of pure individual expression and no one else could have scored a goal quite like it. You can watch it forever and never cease feeling astounded.

It put Clare three points ahead. Cork were level within six minutes but the tide had turned against them. They were hanging on now. Five minutes from time a third point from

Diarmuid Ryan, having a colossal game at wing-back, put Clare three clear. Cork looked spent. We appeared to have a winner.

Things weren't going to be that simple. With a minute left of normal time a long ball from Patrick Collins broke behind the Clare full-back line and Cork sub Robbie O'Flynn appeared to have a clear run on goal. When David McInerney tripped him the obvious decision was a black card for McInerney and a penalty for Cork. It was an open and shut case but the sight of referee Johnny Murphy running in to speak with his umpires made me think he wouldn't give it. Such consultations are often the prelude to a referee bottling out of a big decision and that's what happened this time. Murphy merely gave a free which Patrick Horgan put over the bar.

There were claims afterwards that the presence of covering players in the vicinity meant O'Flynn didn't really have the clear goalscoring opportunity required under the rules. The truth is that this was an even clearer black card offence than the one committed by Kyle Hayes in Cork.

There's a view that you shouldn't really criticise referees for getting things wrong because it's a hard job. But if you praise Seán Stack for having the bravery to make a big call, you can't really ignore Murphy's decision. The easy route for Stack in Páirc Uí Chaoimh would have been to award Cork a free in. He wouldn't have received that much criticism for not applying a rarely used rule. Cork would have been knocked out of the championship, Hayes would have been praised for being 'streetwise' and Limerick would probably have gone on to win five in a row. Stack's courage changed the course of the championship.

At least this Murphy mistake was a matter of interpretation. Worse was to follow but his charitable attitude towards McInerney, who might also have got a second yellow card and been sent off, didn't seem to matter so much when Cork hit two more points at the start of injury-time to draw level. With Clare looking nervy, might the Rebels sneak it after all?

Enter Kelly, snapping up a puck-out, shipping a challenge and, with three defenders around him, striking a shot over his shoulder and over the bar from fifty yards. It was truly a point to win an All-Ireland final. But in the very last seconds Clare gave away another free and Horgan pointed to bring us into extra-time. Phew.

Things were level again after the first half of extra-time. O'Flynn hit a great point to put Cork ahead just eighteen seconds after the restart. Clare equalised and it was nip and tuck for the next few minutes before our next turning point. He'd only come on three minutes from the end of normal time but O'Flynn ended up being involved in an inordinate amount of big moments.

Six minutes into the second half he raced through on the right and found himself with a clear shot in a similar position to that from which Rodgers had scored his goal at the other end. Taking a point was an option but O'Flynn went for goal and

Quilligan saved. The forward ended up with the worst of both worlds, neither a goal nor a point.

Two minutes later Kelly came down like a wolf on the fold to knock the ball away from one Cork player. The Rebels recovered the ball but Kelly swooped again. One flick intercepted a handpass, the second steered the sliotar round an opponent, the third put it in his hand and the fourth sent it between the posts. The bravura of it all suggested a man enjoying himself to the hilt. It had never been harder not to cheer in the press box.

It was a score to put heart in your own team and break the hearts of the opposition and Clare added two points to once more be in pole position entering injury-time. Horgan pulled one back with a free and then with the game surely in its last seconds Cork won a free deep in their own half and just a point between the teams.

Collins launched the ball long and O'Flynn caught it. He seemed a cert to score the equaliser but put his shot wide. The whistle blew immediately afterwards and in a game full of superlative moments the sub had apparently perpetrated one of the great All-Ireland final misses.

It quickly became apparent that this wasn't the full story. We'd barely left our press box seats when photos emerged showing that as O'Flynn took the ill-fated shot his jersey was being pulled by Clare corner-back Conor Leen. This wasn't a slight tug, O'Flynn's jersey was stretched far enough away from his body for someone to put their head in the gap. Leen gleefully admitted the following day that he'd committed the foul and would do it again in the same situation. Defending is often about what you can get away with. One of the greatest games of all time had ultimately been decided by a refereeing error. It wasn't a player but the ref who'd perpetrated a miss for the ages. There should have been a draw and a replay.

It was hard to accept that such a great game could hinge on this. There was something almost offensive about the idea. It felt like an affront to our notions of sporting justice. We like to see big matches as moral tales where everyone gets what they deserve. We prefer the clear-cut, all-loose-ends-tied-up finish of an Agatha Christie whodunnit to the ambiguity of *Zodiac*. That was why so many people pretended the missed call was not central but peripheral to the outcome.

There was only one good reason for thinking this way. If you come from Clare you're absolutely entitled to gloss over the decision. I'd do likewise if I was from Clare. No added justification is necessary.

Other rationalisations were considerably less impressive. There was the one which said you can't pin the outcome of the game on one decision as many other things happened along the way. This is technically correct but why then do people still rail against such injustices as Thierry Henry's handball against Ireland, Neil Back's illegal steal from Peter Stringer in the Heineken Cup final or Diego Maradona's fisted goal against England? Other stuff happened in those games too. The injustice may even have been lesser because Ireland, Munster and England had ample time to redress it. Whereas the final whistle blew straight after O'Flynn's wide. There was no comeback. The decision was final.

In this it most resembled the blatantly illegal goal which Joe Sheridan scored for Meath in the 2010 Leinster final against Louth, the allowing of which remains by some distance the worst refereeing decision in the history of Irish sport. Yet even then people argued that Louth should quickly move on and accept that these things happen. They'd bounce back all the stronger for the experience. They didn't, of course.

I even remember people suggesting that Louth were ultimately to blame because their defence should have cleared the ball before Joe Sheridan dived for glory and Martin Sludden looked the other way. This kind of victim-blaming resurfaced after the hurling final with the argument that even if O'Flynn was being fouled he should have scored anyway. But without Leen holding his jersey O'Flynn could have taken another couple of steps to gain crucial extra space. He'd have been better balanced if he wasn't being tugged backwards. The shot would have been an entirely different one.

It was a silly argument. Peter Shilton could have been quicker off his line, Peter Stringer should have been a bit more alert, Paul McShane might have cleared the ball before it came to Henry. None of those things would have mattered if the referee had made the right decision. They're irrelevant. The ref isn't entitled to impose arbitrary punishments for poor technique.

Another argument is that Clare deserved to win anyway because they were the better team on the day. They certainly were but they let Cork off the hook as they'd let Limerick off the hook in previous matches by going into their shell in the final few minutes. The ref also isn't entitled to make decisions on the basis of poetic justice.

Johnny Murphy didn't do any of these things. He just didn't see the foul. People have said this is understandable because they were in the stands and didn't see it either. The important phrase there is 'in the stands'. The referee isn't in the stands, he's on the pitch right next to the players. He's not a spectator, he's a man whose only job is to ensure both teams get fair play. He didn't do that.

A few Cork people indulged in ostentatious displays of sportsmanship and said they had no complaints. It was suggested that the inherent nobility of hurling fans meant it was beneath them to worry about something as trivial as a refereeing decision which decided the outcome of an All-Ireland final.

Each to their own. But I'm not a Cork fan and I'm not Hurling Man. I'm a sports journalist. I don't think it's a particularly important job but if it's to mean anything at all you have to say what you saw. You have to be honest and you can't get carried away by the emotion of big occasions. You can't not mention the significance of Murphy's decision because, in the words of Myles na gCopaleen, 'Do spile sé an effect – it spoils the effect.'

I might be accused of making a big deal out of the moment because I have a soft spot for Cork. Once you enter the press box such considerations hold little sway. You go into another zone. I watched the final side by side with a man I've known for decades, an excellent GAA reporter who's also a passionate fan of Clare hurling. You wouldn't have known to look at either of us which team we were partial towards. His only flicker of emotion came when the final whistle blew and he said, almost in a whisper and partly to himself, 'I can't believe I've seen Clare win four All-Irelands.' Then, as his fellow county men celebrated wildly, he got back to work. That's the drill.

Clare deserved an All-Ireland title. They had Kelly, they had O'Donnell and perhaps most importantly they had Brian Lohan. Few managers had ever taken charge of a county team in less promising circumstances. Clare was roiled by internecine warfare between different factions on the county board. Those involved were making a show of themselves – there were allegations of abusive phone calls and threats of getting the guards involved. Lohan was entitled to believe that a cohort within the county wished to see him fail. At one stage it was proposed to set up a committee to examine the state of the game in Clare whose members might include Davy Fitzgerald, the manager of a rival county and a contender to replace Lohan. Davy's father Pat was county board secretary. The Clare management job wasn't just a poisoned chalice but one with acid smeared on the handle for good measure. Lohan looked like a dead manager walking during his first couple of years in the job.

Yet after the disappointments of the 2022, 2023 and 2024 Munster finals and the 2022 and 2023 All-Ireland semi-finals he had steered the Banner to an All-Ireland title no one had predicted at the start of the season. Who could begrudge Lohan success after all the obstacles he'd had to overcome? Clare were worthy champions.

But it should still have been a free.

24

Wake Me Up Before You GAAGO

IN THE PRESS ROOM AT HALF-TIME THERE WAS A
stunned shock at what we'd just witnessed in the All-Ireland
football final between Galway and Armagh. The New York
Stock Exchange on the morning of the Wall Street Crash
probably felt a bit like this. Or the engine room of the *Titanic*
on its night to remember.

'Icebergs, bloody hell.'

Even Marty Morrissey, that most incorrigible of enthusiasts,
was grim when we chatted.

Not only was this the last match of the 2024 football
championship but it was also the last match of its kind that
there'd ever be. Gaelic football had blown it. We shuffled out of
the room and back towards our seats like the cast of *Blackadder*

heading over the top in the final episode. The second half wouldn't be any better.

My mother had become very invested in seeing Galway win an All-Ireland, sixty years after watching the team she'd always regard as the benchmark of football excellence win the first of three in a row. She planted a large flag outside her house and kept telling me on the phone, as if I might be able to pass on the information to the man above, 'It would mean a lot to me if they were to win this.'

Just before leaving Skibbereen the previous morning I'd seen Don Davis in the SuperValu coffee shop. Twenty-five years previously he'd played for Cork in an All-Ireland final against Meath. In 1993 he'd had an outstanding game against Derry, setting up two goals.

He'd lost both games but even playing in them was something most players never achieved. Probably no one who's ever played or watched football and hurling hasn't wondered at some stage what it would be like to wake up one morning and think, 'I'm playing in an All-Ireland final today.' Don Davis knew. The rest of us could only imagine.

Even being there to watch one seems a pretty big deal. The atmosphere around Croke Park before the football final was actually more electric than it had been before the hurling final. Armagh were famously boisterous supporters and had the star turn of the day with a guy wearing an orange version of one of those Nudie suits popular with more flamboyant country music stars, but Galway were on song too. The atmosphere was charged with expectation. The stage was set.

Then the football started and sapped the life out of everyone. You could almost hear the crowd gradually deflating like a tyre with a slow puncture. The huge, wild outpourings of noise which had greeted the teams' arrival on the pitch, the parade and the throw-in ebbed away to be replaced by the subdued murmur which had become the staple soundtrack to football matches in this year of dross. It was the sound of 82,000 people trying their best to stay interested as the teams took the heat out of the occasion like soccer sides seeking to quiet a partisan crowd in a European tie away from home. It was the sound of people at the opera trying to stay awake till one of the big numbers came up. These days football was all recitative and no arias.

Galway held the ball for two minutes on their first possession and Paul Conroy scored a point. They held it for three minutes on their second and Liam Silke scored a point. Armagh scored their first two points much more easily, flying down the pitch for Oisín Conaty to twice find the target. Conaty, a former Irish League soccer player with Portadown and Linfield, was probably the attacking player of the year, the one ballplayer consistently prospering in a desert for flair forwards. The kid was a breath of fresh air in a suffocating game.

Galway looked weighed down by the favourites mantle and tentative in everything they did. Maddeningly deliberate at the best of times, their build-up play was silting up. Armagh were sharper and quicker when they had the ball but spent most of their time defending in depth and trying to play on the counter-attack.

The combination of these two approaches resulted in stasis. Players spent a lot of time jogging around at half-pace, passing the ball sideways and backwards and generally doing the football equivalent of treading water. Why was it such a peculiarly terrible spectacle? Why did it make neutral spectators feel so outraged and short-changed? There had been notoriously bad All-Ireland finals before, Kerry against Roscommon in 1980, Dublin against Galway in 1983, Meath v. Cork in 1988. The Tyrone–Armagh decider I'd written about in 2003 had been pretty dour too.

It wasn't the same. The 1980 and 1983 finals had been preceded by two of the great semi-finals, Kerry's win over Offaly and Dublin's over Cork, a pair of exuberant shoot-outs yielding fourteen goals between them. 1988 and 2003 were dull deciders in far from vintage years but still somehow not as apocalyptically bad as today's offering.

Lack of intensity was the big problem. The 1988 and 2003 games had the consolations of physicality: a lot of challenges were going in and a lot of battles being fought even if the football wasn't particularly open. Now players avoided bringing the ball into a tackle and spent long stretches passing back and forth in front of the opposition defence. Whereas hurlers had to be alert every second of the game because they never knew when the ball would arrive in their area, much of the football final looked like the teams were taking a breather. The runs were half-paced, the passes were short, the pace was funereal. The GAA, so fond of describing hurling as the fastest field game in the world, seemed to also be in possession of the slowest one.

It was 0–6 each at half-time. There'd been a great long-range point for both sides, Paul Conroy scoring Galway's and Ben Crealey Armagh's. More significantly, Shane Walsh had kicked two scorable frees wide.

For a glorious, and sadly deceptive, twelve minutes at the start of the second half it looked like we'd been too hasty in our judgements. 1–7 was scored, another great long point from Conroy, a fine solo effort from the admirable Conaty, an effort which got Shane Walsh off the mark from play and the game's only goal. It came in the forty-seventh minute, less than a minute after Kieran McGeeney had sent on Stefan Campbell. Campbell had a maverick air about him he liked to express himself and take risks in possession. He wasn't physically cut-out for the constant chasing back into defence which was de rigueur for modern forwards but he soloed the ball with the confidence of a man who can make it do anything he wants.

His very first act on the pitch was to take a pass from Crealey, burst past John Maher and from the left of the goals fist a ball which floated across the square. Was it a point effort dropped short or a canny set-up? Either way Connor Gleeson should have cut it out. Instead the big man, who'd redeemed himself in Pearse Stadium, unredeemed himself by hesitating long enough for Aaron McKay, up from full-back and allowed to run free by Shane Walsh, to beat him to the ball and flick it into the net.

Great, you thought, this is exactly what the game needed. This'll really set things up. It didn't. It killed them off. There was almost half an hour remaining and there'd be just five points scored in that period as the game degenerated into a frantic mess. Armagh would score just two of those points. Their reaction to going ahead was to retreat, defend en masse and try to sit on the lead for the rest of the game.

It was a huge gamble which almost certainly wouldn't have worked against Dublin or Kerry or even Donegal. Ceded the initiative, those counties would have found the necessary scores. Galway were different. They made hard work of scoring at the best of times and depended a lot on the individual brilliance of Walsh, Damien Comer or Rob Finnerty to turbo-charge their pedestrian build-up. But Finnerty had gone off injured in the eleventh minute, for the second final in a row they were unable to find a way to get the ball to Comer, and Walsh was having a nightmare for the ages. It was like the dark doppelganger of his sublime performance in the 2022 All-Ireland final, a display which had people seriously discussing whether he might be up there with David Clifford at the pinnacle of forward accomplishment.

Now Walsh endured a footballing dark night of the soul. A horrible sliced wide in the fifty-seventh minute, a kickable free dropped short in the sixty-second minute, a growing sensation of a player pushing too hard because he felt his form deserting him. When Walsh stood over a borderline scorable free at the start of injury-time no one in the stadium expected him to land it. He didn't look like he did himself. This free dropped short too. Watching Walsh felt like an infringement of his privacy at this stage. There was a kind of pain about his performance which made it difficult to witness. He was not playing but drowning.

Galway were a point down when he missed that free and they were still that point down at the end. Armagh had won an All-Ireland title even more unexpected than Clare's. No one had foreseen this at the start of the season. Or even midway through it when after their Ulster final penalty shoot-out defeat some eejit predicted that 'Armagh will never win anything under Kieran McGeeney'.

That was me. It wasn't an uncommon opinion. A faction in Armagh had even attempted to replace McGeeney after the previous year's championship. I got it spectacularly wrong, partly because of the habit of presuming that the team that won had got it all right and the team that lost got it all wrong. This desire for a neat ending extended to insisting that the team which prevails in a penalty shoot-out deserved to win the game beforehand. You see that all the time in soccer. We can't bear the idea that the penalty shoot-out is an almost entirely arbitrary way of deciding the destination of even the most major honours and that in 1994, 2006 and 2022, Italy, France and France again deserved to win the World Cup final just as much as Brazil, Italy and Argentina.

The same calculus was employed when Gaelic football adopted the shoot-out. Armagh had lost four of them and on each occasion the winners, particularly Derry and Donegal in the previous two Ulster finals, had been lauded for their winning mentality and Armagh derided as nearly-men. We'd extracted the wrong moral from these games. Armagh weren't losers, because they hadn't lost any of them. In fact that refusal to lose, especially when looking second best against Galway and Derry, was the elephant in the room. We pretended penalties were a form of justice rather than a game of chance.

That wasn't the only way I'd been wrong about Armagh. I'd insisted that their only chance of winning the All-Ireland was by freeing the better angels of their nature and favouring adventure over caution. Armagh could play sparkling attacking football. Against Donegal in 2022 and Derry in 2024 they'd been absolutely exhilarating when cutting loose and scoring 3–17 on both occasions. They possessed more gifted forwards than anyone apart from possibly Dublin and Kerry. It seemed their best way to success would be to make the most of that firepower. In the final they'd taken the opposite route. It seemed symbolic that their very best attacker, Conor Turbitt, was taken off in the forty-sixth minute. There was no room for him in such a grimly utilitarian game.

You can't argue with an All-Ireland title. Yet Armagh looked four or five points better than Galway on the day and might have won by that margin had they kicked on after McKay's goal. In lying back after taking the lead, they were showing the same kind of caution which had backfired against them in the Ulster final. The two teams that eventually won the All-Irelands actually did so while making the same mistakes which had cost them dear in the past. Clare had lost their composure in the final few minutes and Armagh had gone into their shell. This time it didn't matter because the opposition wasn't strong enough to take advantage.

For Armagh fans, any discussions of the merits of their victory is beside the point. One of the county's supporters wrote to inform me that 'history is written by the winners', which, though I see his point, betrays a touching ignorance of recent trends in historical publishing.

Yet the All-Ireland they won was an odd one. Just how odd became apparent when fourteen of the fifteen football All-Stars turned out to be first-time winners (Tyrone keeper Niall Morgan being the exception). Initial years aside, this had only happened once before, in 1987. The failure of almost all the game's established stars to shine gave the championship a year zero feeling. No championship had made so little impact on the national sporting conversation. It was over and then it was gone.

The appetite for change created by the terrible nature of the 2024 championship meant that the proposals of Jim Gavin's Football Review Committee would be greeted as a rescue mission for football.

The FRC decided that they had a choice between radicalism and redundancy and shortly after the end of the season came up with a list of suggestions which would fundamentally change the nature of the game rather than just tinker around the edges. The Railway Cup games in which they were trialled for the first time attracted an enormous amount of public interest.

These changes, in particular the requirement to keep three players in the opposition half at all times and for kick-outs to go beyond an arc forty yards from goal, would profoundly change football. There'd also be massively increased penalties for the dissent, gamesmanship and time-wasting which had been almost as damaging to the game as a spectacle as negative tactics. The GAA had grown tired of waiting for managers and players to self-police and decided to impose virtue on them instead. It was an admission that the game had hit a dead end. It was an admission of defeat. Football as we knew it had run out of road. Welcoming the changes, Niall Morgan and Monaghan keeper Rory Beggan used the word 'boring' in describing the game. Everyone had stopped pretending. The FRC's recommendations were passed overwhelmingly at Congress. The 2025 championship would be so different from its predecessor as to seem a different game.

For the moment Armagh are champions and McGeeney has been utterly vindicated. I found him a fascinating figure because he espoused the kind of macho values which had taken such a battering in recent years. He'd trained for almost a decade and a half with Conor McGregor's trainer John Kavanagh and earned a black belt in Brazilian jiu-jitsu. McGregor had sparred with McGeeney and described him as an 'animal', which was probably the finest compliment he could imagine. McGeeney said things like, 'Fighting is probably the rawest form of sport, in the sense that you could walk in a man but you could be very much less of a man when you walk out.'

Not many people spoke like this anymore outside of Cormac McCarthy novels. The association of fighting and manliness sounded anachronistic and antediluvian. It struck an odd note at a time when the Gaelic Players Association ran wellness programmes for its members and the GAA had a mental health charter. Manning up was no longer seen as the best option at times of trouble.

Some people were cynical about the GAA's embrace of such issues. A gay friend of my daughter quipped, 'It's great to see the guys who bullied the rest of us for years in school suddenly tweeting about mental health.' I thought the GAA's interest and that of the players involved was genuine. It might lead to less bullying in the future for one thing.

The world in which the old macho values were useful had largely disappeared. They may have served some purpose in helping men survive wars or endure conditions in coal mines or steel works but seem outmoded now. Yet perhaps one area where they might still come in handy is managing a football or hurling squad. The environment has changed somewhat but it's still macho to an extent rarely encountered in ordinary life. McGeeney's MMA-derived insight that 'when someone's trying to kill you, there's always a way out' might sound like wisdom in that context.

The problem arises when the person trying to kill you is yourself. One reason the GPA and the GAA are focused on mental health issues is that surveys have shown above-average levels of depression, anxiety, gambling addiction, binge-drinking and stress among inter-county players. Well-known players have come out and talked about their experiences in this area. It seems pretty clear that in these cases machismo does more harm than good.

I'm one of the least macho men you could meet. I can't drive, I've never been in a fight and I know the words of three dozen Stephen Sondheim songs. Yet what did me more damage than anything else in my struggle with anxiety was a refusal to ask for help or admit how bad the problem was. I thought it would show weakness. I thought it would be unmanly so I tried to man up and the problem just got worse. Some things which work in the dressing room and on the field may prove a real menace for players in everyday life. The macho code might suit some men but it's toxic for a lot of others.

It's also toxic for those who have to deal with them, women in particular. The grimmest aspects of the macho code were laid bare when Kavanagh appeared in the High Court as an apparent show of support for McGregor before the fighter was found liable in the civil case taken against him by Nikita Hand, the woman who alleged that he'd raped her. The lads were sticking by each other no matter what. The year would end with the arrest of an Armagh player for an alleged sexual assault carried out during the trip to the USA the team had taken to celebrate their All-Ireland victory. Two days earlier, former Irish under-20 rugby international Denis Coulson had been one of three players jailed for the gang rape of a young woman in Bordeaux.

Managers could not be blamed for such incidents. At a time when online porn, influencers in the Andrew Tate mould and role models like McGregor encouraged new manifestations of the old-school misogyny, the battle for the souls of young men was not confined to sport. Yet there were plenty of people outside the sporting bubble who felt that the traditional ethos of team sport was part of the solution rather than part of the problem.

This was not entirely fair. The GAA has always reflected society as a whole and plenty of players didn't conform to the stereotypical notion of the bone-headed macho jock. Tyrone's Conor Meyler, who'd been shortlisted for Footballer of the Year in 2021, was working on a PhD 'on the areas of sport, leadership and gender with a focus on the integration of Gaelic games'.

Yet he'd 'been abused a few times when playing with Tyrone over this. Players making a jibe about it, questioning my sexuality, giving me homophobic abuse. Then there'd be fellas going, "What are you doing here? You should be playing with the Tyrone ladies." Just stupid stuff'.

The struggle continues.

25

Another City

ON THE MORNING OF THE FOOTBALL FINAL I'D been walking through Rathmines when the sound of hymn-singing drifted towards me across the grounds of St Mary's College. I followed it and discovered a religious service taking place in the chapel where they'd no doubt once given thanks for five Leinster Senior Cup wins and the God-given talent of Paul Dean, Denis Hickie and Johnny Sexton.

I seemed to be the only non-Indian in the congregation but the service was recognisably a Christian one. These were members of the St Gregorios Jacobite Syriac Orthodox Church which traced its faith back to people from the state of Kerala converted by St Thomas the Apostle in the year AD 52. Their mass is known as the Holy Qurbana and includes some of the oldest prayers in Christianity. It is very beautiful, making great use of singing and chanting in the native Keralan tongue of

Malayalam, and very long; I stood for two and a half hours. It seemed a marvellous thing to stumble across on a suburban Sunday morning 5,400 miles from Kerala.

I'd stood on my own a few seats away from anyone else but when the time to offer a sign of peace arrived two men went out of their way to include me. The Qurbana sign of peace involves opening both hands to allow the other person to place their hand between them. I made a better go at it the second time. The grace of the singing and chanting, the sense of communal joy, the bright clothes of the worshippers combined to give me a feeling of aesthetic bliss, of discovery, of happiness. I'd gone to these services out of curiosity but what I'd ended up getting was pleasure and a kind of enlightenment. As I walked away from St Mary's, the city seemed a different place. I thought of an English reviewer of *The Famished Road* by Ben Okri who said that when they finished it they expected to come outside and see angels sitting on the trees. It was that kind of feeling. These services had enlarged the city for me. It seemed charged with potential.

I was hungry for the city that summer. It was as if a dam had burst within me, the decades of reclusion giving way to an enthusiastic curiosity about everything which I hadn't felt in years. Everything about Dublin was interesting to me, most of all the world of the immigrants who'd changed the monocultural city of my younger days almost beyond recognition.

If you wanted to encapsulate the spirit of Immigrant Dublin there are few better places than the Moore Street Mall where I had lunch several times before proceeding to Croke Park. There's an almost surreptitious feel to the entrance through a small door off Parnell Street. You pass a display of flavoured vapes, take an elevator and find yourself in a subterranean space devoted to the needs of those who've come here from elsewhere. There are Georgian, Brazilian, Bolivian, Balkan, Indian and Korean restaurants, a Polish supermarket, places to send money home and to transport your belongings overseas. It's not a fancy place; the chairs and tables in the restaurants give them the look of work canteens, the roof is low and the lighting a little on the harsh side. I love it. It may be my favourite place in Dublin. I've never had anything other than a great meal here though in fairness I'm a 'fine feedie' rather than a foodie. The mall strikes a chord with me. It suits me. I like to see people from all over come in here from the city and visibly relax because nothing brings you back home like the food from home. It's where the nation under our feet without whom the economy of the city would collapse comes to shelter from the storm and hang loose. It's a place where people who are hustling hard to make a living take a time out. Irish pubs on London street corners used to have the same vibe. I feel oddly at home there.

In the Sabor Nordestino Brazilian restaurant I had a fine

steak the afternoon of the football final. With that, a big heap of beans and a can of guarana I was set up for the day.

The morning after the match I went to the Dublin Mosque on the South Circular Road. I'd contacted Imam Yahya Al-Hussein to ask if that'd be OK (there being no service that day) and he said fire ahead.

The Dublin Mosque had once been a nineteenth-century Presbyterian church. A mosque since 1983, it's Dublin's original of the species. I walked in past a couple of collection boxes, one for Syria and one for Palestine, and met a cheerful, balding man in his sixties with a bucket of water in his hand.

'I should probably show you around and give you a talk about the meaning of Islam,' he said, 'but I'm really busy cleaning. Do you mind?'

I said no and asked if I should my take my shoes off.

'If you don't mind. You can go into the prayer hall but upstairs is for the ladies ... exclusively.'

Accompanying the final statement with a grin, he moved off to commence mopping operations. There was only one person in the prayer room at this hour of the day, a young man prostrating himself and praying in the direction of Mecca, indicated by a niche in the centre of the right-hand wall. Next to it was a digital screen with a list of the day's prayer times. The combination of high roof and thick carpet lent the room a cocoon quality. Just being there felt like an act of meditation. This was another refuge, a space separate from the city. I lingered a while, read the list of Islamic laws on the wall and picked up a couple of information leaflets on the way out.

The cheery factotum was still mopping but a couple of girls in headscarves were chasing each other round his nice clean floor at top speed. He shrugged his shoulders, mopped on and bade me goodbye.

I wondered if the girls had been to the recent summer camp which a poster on the wall told me had included kayaking, rock climbing, ziplining, archery and laser combat. It was run by the Muslim Sisters of Éire, a remarkable group who for over a decade had been providing food to around 500 homeless people every Friday night outside the GPO. If anyone was entitled to a bit of ziplining and laser combat it was the Sisters.

Further down the South Circular I went into a Bulgarian shop. I told the woman it was the first Bulgarian shop I'd ever been in.

'It is just shop.'

'But with Bulgarian stuff in it.'

'It is just shop like anywhere else. Nothing any different.'

Her case was slightly weakened by the fact that I was holding a large block of Bulgarian cheese with a cute picture of a farmer and a goat on the front of it, but I saw her point. Two doors down I bought a big bag of excellent Iranian dates from a halal shop. The nearest Luas stop was Fatima, a name which back in the eighties symbolised the heroin epidemic afflicting the city. The idea that one day immigrants would flock to this part of the city, or to any part of the city or the country for that matter, would have seemed outlandish. That Ireland was a place you left.

As I waited for the train in Heuston a well-dressed woman in her sixties started talking to me. She had the air of someone bursting to tell you something.

'There's thirty-four nationalities in the school in Ballyhaunis,' she said, 'so I upped sticks and moved to Westport.'

Ballyhaunis to Westport. White flight wasn't what it used to be. I mentioned the Halal Meats factory in Ballyhaunis and how my brother had worked for a short while in their factory in Ballaghaderreen. Ireland's first purpose-built mosque was the one in Ballyhaunis for employees of the factory, owned by the Pakistani businessman Sher Rafique. Halal Meats had been a rare bright spot in the dark industrial landscape of the eighties.

'My father was a farmer. They all had the height of respect for the Halals. They paid the farmers on time and no nonsense.'

As a kid I'd also thought Halal was the name of the guy who owned the factory.

An old woman from Caherciveen wearing a woolly hat sat beside me on the train. She offered me a small chocolate bar out of a plastic bag filled with them and wondered if I'd been at the final. She had.

'I've been at fifty-three football finals. And fifty-three hurling finals. I haven't missed one, except for during Covid.'

I told her I'd gone to a game every weekend this summer and listed the places I'd been.

'You're a single man, then?'

'I'm separated. I have three daughters. I spend a lot of time with them.'

'They must miss you when you're away all the same.'

Her voice was disapproving. I saw how it might look from her angle. Jack-the-lad traipsing up and down the country to matches without worrying too much about his kids. Not a bother on him. We never really know what's going on with anyone.

She had a habit of briefly dozing off as she spoke. Eventually she fell asleep. After a while, her hat fell off and I saw the stubble which was starting to grow back on her head. No. We never really know.

On the day I visited the Dublin Mosque a teenage boy stabbed three young girls to death in the English town of Southport. The next day crowds laid siege to the Southport Mosque. Over the following week other mosques were targeted during riots which spread to several English cities and injured hundreds of people. They also spread to Belfast where a café owned by a Muslim immigrant was set on fire.

Much play was made of the fact that the protests had been sparked by false social media claims that the attacker was a Muslim asylum seeker. This seemed to inadvertently suggest that if he had been a Muslim the people who'd attacked the mosque might have had a point. This idea that immigrants are a kind of hostage community who should be held collectively responsible for the misdeeds of any of their number wasn't new. I'd been at the receiving end of it myself.

The IRA had engaged in a sporadic bombing campaign in England during my four years there and I encountered a small number of people who apparently felt all Irish people in London bore some responsibility. This generally manifested itself in nothing more serious than snide comments, the odd hectoring demand for contrition and rhetorical questions about whether you were proud of something which really had nothing to do with you.

This stuff didn't make me feel physically threatened but it was unpleasant. There was a British Rail employee at the station where I took the train to work who kept at it and I dreaded the sight of her. Underpinning it was a belief that, even if you didn't agree with the bombings, you weren't sorry enough. It was the attitude Paul Brady captured in the song 'Nothing but the Same Old Story'.

These days others were being persecuted by this warped notion of collective culpability. Ordinary Muslims were saddled with the rap for the deeds of Islamist terrorists, Russians for those of Vladimir Putin, Jews for those of Benjamin Netanyahu, immigrants as a whole ended up being abused, threatened or even assaulted in supposed retaliation for crimes committed by immigrants.

We'd had our own riot the previous November, also sparked by a knife attack on young children. The centre of it was Parnell Street which many people probably dismissed as the kind of grim inner-city location where you could expect trouble. Yet Parnell Street was to an extent a monument to the benefits of immigration. It contains some genuinely excellent restaurants, Indian Tiffins whose masala dosa (pancakes stuffed with potatoes and chillis) might be the best thing you can eat for breakfast in the city, the Pho Kim Vietnamese restaurant, the Kimchi Korean restaurant, the Chinese Lee's Charming Noodles. There are African and Brazilian barber shops, Asian grocery stores and a horde of other immigrant businesses.

Parnell Street might not be pretty but it's not decaying like it was a few decades back. I walked through it several times on my way to Croke Park and passed by Mountjoy Square Park which tended to be largely empty when I lived in Dublin. Last summer it was always packed. There were Indian, African, Romanian and Irish parents too playing with their kids and games of basketball going on. This is not gentrification but organic regeneration. The tenacity with which immigrant-owned businesses have clung to their berths on Parnell Street and elsewhere in the city is admirable. Those involved have created one of the great unsung success stories of modern Ireland, one which deserves to be celebrated and one which seems very much in the Irish grain. We pride ourselves in siding with the underdog, after all.

Those arguing the pro-immigration case tend to invoke the example of Irish emigration during the Famine. We don't need to go that far back or be so dramatic. The year after I went to England, 1989, 2 per cent of the Irish population emigrated. Those were the years of Jim Fahy interviewing tearful emigrants home for Christmas at Knock Airport, of The Wolfe Tones singing 'Flight of Earls' and The Saw Doctors singing 'N17', of bumping into people you knew from home in Tube stations, of 'there'll soon be no young people left in this country'. My Uncle Ned who'd emigrated to England in the fifties and come back in the sixties spent a decade and a half in Boston working illegally on another man's passport. We weren't fleeing famine or war – we were going to make a better living for ourselves as most people who come to Ireland are doing today. Having done it myself I couldn't begrudge someone else doing the same thing. If there really were children of thirty-four nationalities in the school in Ballyhaunis, good luck to them all. That number wasn't an indictment of modern Ireland. It was a tribute to it.

26

The Root of All Good

IN 2003, MY *ROAD TO CROKER* ENDED AT THE
football final between Tyrone and Armagh. I should have known
better. I'd been at the 1998 ladies' football final replay between
Waterford and Monaghan – a classic match illuminated by two
extraordinary individual performances from the former's full-
forward Geraldine O'Ryan and the latter's midfield star Edel
Byrne – and at the following year's decider when Mayo had
scored a massive upset win over a Waterford team seeking a
sixth title in nine years. It still didn't occur to me to include
the 2003 final between Dublin and Mayo in the book. That
might stand as a motto for decades of general neglect: 'Women's
sport – it didn't occur to us.' *Mea culpa*.

The 16,421 crowd at the drawn 1998 final was viewed as a

major advance for the game but it was only the start. The 20,000 barrier was exceeded in 2005 when Cork played Galway. Ten years later Cork and Galway topped the 30,000 mark and just two years after that a crowd of 46,286 at the Dublin–Mayo decider sent shockwaves through Irish sport. The momentum was unstoppable and in 2019 Dublin and Galway drew an astounding 56,114 fans.

That figure deserves putting into perspective. It was the second biggest crowd at any women's sporting event in the world that year, falling just short of the 57,900 which attended the women's soccer World Cup final in France earlier that summer. The women's rugby World Cup final played in Ireland two years before had drawn 17,115 fans. The figure for the 2019 women's Champions League final between Lyon and Barcelona was 19,487, and that for the women's FA Cup final between Manchester City and West Ham United at Wembley was 43,264. The Croke Park crowd also surpassed 52,432 at the previous Olympic women's soccer final between Sweden and Germany at the Maracaña Stadium in Rio de Janeiro.

Let's leave other women's sporting events aside. The Dublin–Galway decider was the fourth-best-attended Gaelic football game of the year, beaten only by Dublin's All-Ireland semi-final win over Mayo and their two final meetings with Kerry. It drew almost 25,000 more fans than Kerry's semi-final against Tyrone. Only two hurling matches, the final between Tipperary and Kilkenny and Tipp's semi-final against Wexford, did better. The ladies' football final demanded media attention. It had to occur to you.

This steady rise in attendances largely pre-dated the conscious efforts to heighten the visibility of women's sport connected to a certain extent with the rise of the Me Too movement and a general resurgence of feminist activism. The Ladies Gaelic Football Association was ahead of the curve. In 2017 the IRFU was showered with praise for the sterling promotional work which had attracted record crowds to the women's rugby World Cup. Those record crowds? A combined total of 45,412 for thirty matches.

In the same year that 56,114 watched the ladies' football decider, a record crowd for an Irish women's soccer match attended Ireland's game against Ukraine in Tallaght. The 5,328 was considered a landmark figure. The ladies' football final, which featured the intermediate and junior deciders as curtain-raisers, was in a league of its own. Its growth had been an organic grassroots phenomenon. By 2023 the women's soccer team, which had captured the public imagination by qualifying for that year's World Cup finals, was playing in front of a record 35,944. But ladies' football (women's football would seem preferable but no change of official title appears to be envisaged) had led the way.

Yet the run-up to this year's final between Galway and Kerry was attended by predictions that the crowd might be as low as 35,000. That would be, leaving aside the Covid-affected years of 2020 and 2021, the smallest attendance since 2016. What had gone wrong?

The final was ill-served by the new championship structure where big matches followed each other in a headlong rush towards the end of the season. There'd formerly been a week during which people could digest the hurling final before the build-up for the football final began the week after. In the absence of this week the two games almost bled into each other.

This hectic schedule did a particular disservice to the ladies' football final which previously had a full week to set the scene for its blue-riband event. The sport had always granted the kind of media access which was anathema to its male counterpart and this helped create the special aura of occasion surrounding the ladies' decider. This year was different. The cluttered nature of the schedule meant the ladies' football final build-up got lost to a certain extent. The split season was not its friend.

The problem was hugely exacerbated by the final running slap bang into an Olympics where Irish interest was at an all-time peak. The Paris Games captured the majority of public and media attention. On the Monday before the final Daniel Wiffen had won gold in the 800m freestyle. He'd be going for a double in the 1500m on the afternoon Kerry met Galway. Two days before the final Paul O'Donovan and Fintan McCarthy won gold in the lightweight double sculls. One day before it, Rhys McClenaghan won gold in the pommel horse and Kellie Harrington won an epic lightweight boxing semi-final against arch-rival Beatriz Ferreira. It would have been hard for any sport to compete with the excitement surrounding these achievements. Ladies' football was edged out of the limelight in a way it had never been before.

I hoped the crowd estimate might be unduly pessimistic. No one had seen 2017's huge jump in attendance coming. On Sunday morning in Galway a long queue of young female football fans had already assembled when I arrived for the train. It was a dirty, wet morning. As I'd left the house my sister had thrown me what looked like a large lump of plastic sheeting but was apparently a rain poncho.

No one, we were told, would be getting on board this train without a pre-booked seat. Or almost no one.

She plonked herself down on the seat next to me, a woman in her sixties with an air of barely contained exasperation.

'I had such an argument. He told me I couldn't get on the train unless I had a seat booked. I asked him for his name and he wouldn't give it to me. He let me on in the end though.'

A few minutes later a man in his forties, who was with the group of girls in Galway jerseys occupying most of the carriage, stood next to the seat and gazed theatrically at the names illuminated above it.

'Are ye together?' he asked.

'No,' I said, a split second before the woman said, 'Yes,' and glared at me for my obtuseness.

'I think you're sitting in my seat,' he said to her.

She said nothing but gave him a Paddington Bear-style hard stare.

'I'd say I'll be able to find another seat.'

I'd have done the same thing. This lady was not for turning.

'Do you see that field?'

'Sorry?'

'Do you see that field? Well, if Daniel O'Donnell was playing there, I wouldn't go in it to see him.'

Her loyalty was pledged to Nathan Carter.

'I follow Nathan around.'

She had seen him in Leisureland the night before and was looking forward to seeing him in The Marquee in Drumlish with Declan Nerney. A friend had brought her along to see Nathan in the Kilmore in Cavan years back and the die had been cast. She'd worked in a bakery for decades but her great pleasure now was trips all over the country to see her idol. She'd got a good rate in the Galway Bay Hotel, she told me with pride, because they knew her. Her blend of indomitability and vulnerability reminded me of Hyacinth Bouquet in *Keeping Up Appearances*. She knew plenty about Longford football; her nephew was a well-known former inter-county player who I remembered as a secondary school star with St Mel's when I'd worked for the *Longford News* three decades previously. When I mentioned some other country music stars she shuddered as though I'd uttered a blasphemy.

'I don't like him at all,' she'd say. 'It's Nathan for me.'

Declan Nerney was granted a pardon on neighbourly grounds as a fellow north Longfordian. I was well disposed to him myself after his fine turn leading the band at The Shah's wedding in *That They May Face the Rising Sun*. We talked all the way to Athlone, where she'd be getting off to take a bus home and begin planning her next outing. She asked me to bring her bag out onto the platform. As I watched her walk away, I was glad I'd made her acquaintance. She was a woman you don't meet every day.

It was raining when we got to Dublin. I attempted to don the rain poncho and failed miserably. Where did the arms go? Where did you put your head? As the carriage emptied, it kept slipping off and falling to the floor.

'Can I help you with that?' asked a young Indian man.

He completed the operation in seconds. I thanked him.

'It's OK. I'm an engineer.'

At the hotel reception I attempted unsuccessfully to exit from the rain poncho. Some amusement seemed discernible on the face of the young Eastern European woman behind the desk.

'Does this look alright?'

She gave me an appraising glance, as though trying to work out what kind of customer she was dealing with. 'Do you mind dark humour?'

'I don't.'

She looked around, lowered her voice and said, 'You look like a condom.'

I left the rain poncho in the room. It wasn't that far to Croke Park and the weather was clearing up a bit anyway.

Outside Fitzgibbon Street garda station two men and two women scuttled past me at high speed whispering agitatedly. Two guards looked down the street after them. A syringe lay on the ground.

'Don't pick it up,' said the older guard to his companion.

Big GAA matches attract a higher proportion of women fans than big soccer games. They also have the edge when it comes to family groups. Both these tendencies are ramped up considerably at the ladies' football final. The crowd was roughly 75 per cent female and there were numerous buggies, one of which got jammed in a turnstile, and the odd baby strapped to a parent's chest. The final's special atmosphere derives in part from its identity as a de facto festival of the female contribution to the GAA. Spectators are there to watch the game but they're also there to celebrate what it stands for. It's like a giant sporting version of Nollaig na mBan. When I told the woman at the checkout in SuperValu that I was going to the game she'd said, 'Fair play to you,' as though I were performing a charitable function. Perhaps her surprise wasn't that surprising. A survey at the start of 2024 showed that 59 per cent of the Irish population had never attended a women's sporting event. There was a lot done but a lot more to do.

Kerry were favourites. This was their third final in a row. They'd been well beaten by Meath two years ago and by Dublin last year. On the day Kerry had gained revenge on the Royals in the quarter-final, Galway had done them an enormous favour by removing Dublin from the equation. It was a shock on a par with Cork's first win over Limerick in the hurling. The reigning champions had won their five previous games by a combined total of 100 points. But Galway had beaten them and the consensus was that they'd opened the way for Kerry.

They'd opened it for Kerry and for Louise Ní Mhuircheartaigh who was in her seventeenth championship season. There was nothing quite like a Kerry corner-forward and the 33-year-old, skillful, elusive, intelligent, accurate, absolutely comfortable and controlled on the ball, seemed to have issued from the same factory which had produced the likes of Mikey Sheehy, John Egan, Mike Frank Russell, Colm Cooper and Paul Geaney before coming up with a new advanced model in David Clifford. She'd won her first All-Star in 2012 and been one of the best attackers in the game for over a decade, yet unlike her male Kingdom counterparts the Corca Dhuibhne player hadn't an All-Ireland medal to her name. Kerry had made the All-Ireland final in 2012 and lost by nine points to the great Cork team which won all but one of the twelve All-Ireland finals between 2005 and 2016. Cork had been the kind of insurmountable barrier to the Kerry women that Kerry had so often been to the Cork men. When they finally eased off, the slack was taken up by Dublin, Meath and then Dublin again.

Kerry had fancied their chances in the previous year's decider with Ní Mhuircheartaigh tipped to give a bravura performance after scoring 1–10, 1–6 from play, in the semi-final against Mayo. But Dublin had policed her diligently all through the game, and though a total of 1–7, 1–1 from play, was no negligible contribution, she'd cut a frustrated figure for most of the afternoon. Her time was running out.

Galway's first-half performance might have served as a case study in inherited trauma. They played exactly like the men's team had in the second half of their All-Ireland final, moving the ball slowly, missing good chances and generally looking as though something had gone missing since they too had eliminated an All-Ireland-champion Dublin team in the quarter-final.

Kerry were not at their best either and at times looked inhibited by the pressure which came with the possibility of becoming three-time final losers. The big exception was Ní Mhuircheartaigh, relishing the freedom she hadn't been granted the previous year, orchestrating attacks and slotting over the chances which came her way from play and frees. She'd hit six of the points which had Kerry 0–8 to 0–3 coming up to the break. On the stroke of half-time Kerry wing-back Aoife Dillane seemed to shoot for a point but the ball dipped, deceived keeper Dearbhla Gower and ended up in the net.

That was all she wrote. The second half had all the suspense of a whodunnit you've seen before. It really did seem as though the gloom which had settled over Galway after their loss in the men's final had seeped into the bones of their women's side.

The inevitability of the result from a long way out combined with the weather to dampen the atmosphere, and one of the biggest cheers of the afternoon came when a young lad on the other side of the field raised a banner which read 'I'm a Ladies Man'. Yet there was still time for Ó Muircheartaigh to produce one of those moments which makes even a scrappy match worth seeing. A long ball was played down towards her on the right wing. With her marker in close attendance Ó Muircheartaigh let the ball beat her, turned sharply past her now wrong-footed opponent, collected the ball, soloed in from the wing and set up Hannah O'Donoghue for goal number two. It was a classic corner-forward manoeuvre perfectly executed.

O'Donoghue, who'd only come on as a sub in the forty-third minute, was the star of the second half as Ó Muircheartaigh had been of the first. She scored 1–2 and provided the pass which enabled Emma Dineen to score the third goal. Dineen's neat sidestep and calm finish had a Cliffordian flourish to them. O'Donoghue was a biomedical engineer, a somewhat anomalous figure on a team packed with teachers and students. The scientists were having a good summer.

There were three minutes left when Kerry withdrew
Ó Muircheartaigh, solely you suspected so she could get an
individual round of applause which recognised how much
she'd given to the Kingdom over the years. At the sideline she
hopped into the arms of joint manager Declan Quill who, along
with his co-manager Darragh Long, had signed on for one last
shot after the previous year's loss.

It was Kerry's first triumph in thirty-one years but the one-
sided nature of the final left it short on drama. There was another
problem too. The predictions of a 35,000 crowd proved to be
wrong but not in the way I'd hoped. A crowd of 30,340 was the
lowest since 2014 and little more than half of 2019's peak figure.
The wet day couldn't be used as an excuse – the 2019 decider
had been played in even worse weather. Dublin's absence didn't
help but 46,440 people had seen Meath beat Kerry in 2022 and
Galway had been big crowd-pullers in the past.

There was something freakish about the confluence of the
Olympics and the split season. While the former wouldn't be
a factor again till 2028, the latter seemed set to remain. The
LGFA and the Camogie Association had pursued the goal of
union with the GAA for a long time and earlier in the year it
had been revealed that integration would be phased in and fully
completed by 2027. The advantages of such an arrangement
were obvious: improvements in facilities and player welfare
and a check on the tendency of some county boards to treat
the women's game as a secondary consideration. Yet the drop

in the final attendance sounded a warning. By becoming part of the GAA fixture calendar ladies' football had ended up playing its biggest game on the worst possible week in terms of public exposure. Integration would mean little if the women's games ended up as an under-regarded sideshow. The new arrangement would bring challenges as well as opportunities.

As Kerry celebrated and 'I Gotta Feeling' by the Black Eyed Peas reverberated through the stadium, I watched Daniel Wiffen go for gold at 1500m on my phone and found two young women who'd been sitting near me during the match looking over my shoulder. They were English.

'Is that Dan Wiffen?'

'It is.'

We watched as he tried to peg back the American Bobby Finke who'd set off at a world-record pace. Wiffen closed the gap for a while but at some stage after half-way it became apparent that it was opening again. He had to be satisfied with bronze but it had been a good week for the Armagh man. 'We're All-Ireland champions and Olympic gold medallists,' he'd said after winning the 800m. 'What a great county.'

I wished I could tell these English visitors about those amazing figures back in 2019 and the incredible story of how for years the ladies' football final had been one of the best-attended women's sporting events in the world. But this wasn't the day to do it. It may be a blip – the Armagh team who Kerry beat narrowly in the semi-final might have brought a huge number of fans down to see them seek a first ever title, for example. I hoped so. At a time when women's sport was finally getting something approaching its due, it would be sad to see the trailblazers slip behind.

There's a long corridor between the entrance of the Button Factory and the concert space. When I went in that night people were dancing all over that corridor. I dodged between them, opened the door which led to the music and was hit by a blast of heat. Not just the literal kind but the heat of excitement, of creativity, of passionate community. Saulo Fernandes was in town.

It felt like I'd strayed into a particularly joyous family celebration. A star in his native country, Saulo's fame hadn't really crossed over internationally so the audience was almost wholly Brazilian. The experience was very different from going to a world music gig where the majority of the audience are Irish. This felt as if a piece of Brazil had been teleported into Dublin. This was the music in its native habitat. I was having my very own Nathan Carter in the Kilmore moment.

Everyone appeared to know all the words of every song. Everyone danced. They'd been dancing in the corridors, they danced on the balcony, they danced around me, they danced on my toes, they danced with each other, they danced while looking at Saulo on stage as though performing a pas de deux with the singer. The sweat soaked through his white linen jacket as he rose to them and they rose to him. Phones flashed at the front of the stage and occasionally he'd grab one and take photos of the fans before handing it back. From time to time someone would spot somebody they knew in the crowd and there'd be an 'I didn't know you'd be here too, isn't this great' embrace.

It never slowed down. Instead there was a sense of things gaining momentum as they went on and of everything leading to the emotional climax of the final song which began with a chugging reggae-style rhythm, his most famous song, 'Raiz De Todo Bem' (Root of All Good).

The noise from the crowd went up a notch at the opening words to the song, which mention the city of Salvador. It felt as though they were singing along with a national anthem. They were, in a way. This was Saulo's tribute to the great city of his home state, the place where every year four million people went to the biggest party in the world, the Bahia Carnival. He'd twice been voted best singer there. Miguel Gomes, the Portuguese genius who was one of the world's best film directors, had a line in one of his movies about a time when Salvador seemed like the centre of the world. That was in the seventies when Brazil enjoyed one of the greatest explosions of talent in the history of popular music. The only comparable eras were those of US soul music in the sixties and Jamaican reggae in the seventies. Masterpiece after joyous masterpiece and the very best of it came out of Salvador, home city of the two greatest singers, Gilberto Gil and Caetano Veloso, and the greatest band, Novos Baianos. It almost felt like they were in this room too as the crowd bellowed the chorus.

That chorus mentioned Candomblé, a faith traditionally frowned on by the authorities which mixed Catholicism and the African religions preserved by slaves transported to the plantations. So maybe there was a religious element to this night too and among the crowd raising their voices were those for whom this was their testament of belief, as the singing of the Orthodox had been in Harold's Cross. There's almost always a spiritual element to the music that really moves us.

As the crowd drifted away, two young and fairly drunk lads made a beeline for me.

'Did you enjoy?'

'I did. I really enjoyed.'

'Good, good.'

They smiled and one of them clapped me on the back.

Walking back through Temple Bar I thought of a similar night when I'd been their age. The Pogues had played Brixton Academy and there too everyone sang along with the words of every song. The link between Shane McGowan, who was brilliant that night, and his audience was the same as that between Saulo and his. So was the sense of people recreating a corner of home in a foreign city and taking strength from it. The Brazilians might have been famous for their sunny disposition but they made up the majority of the food-delivery cyclists who were being constantly attacked in the city. Dublin was not always easy for them. Salvador was a tougher city still and Brazil's great music was rooted in the culture of communities at the bottom end of the scale. The Brazilian golden age of music coincided with the rule of a military dictatorship which had imprisoned and exiled Gil and Veloso. Samba, axé, reggae, soul, jazz, gospel, all the most joyous music, comes from a place of historical suffering. Perhaps it's because, to paraphrase Samuel Beckett, when you're in the last ditch there's nothing left to do but sing.

I listened to 'Raiz de Todo Bem' at the start of every day writing this book. It put me back in the Button Factory on one of the best nights of my life.

Obrigado, Saulo.

27

Cinema World

THE WOMEN OPPOSITE ME ON THE TRAIN WERE discussing property.

'I'm in Bray,' said a woman in her forties who seemed a decade older than her companions. 'I wish it would gentrify faster. It needs some restaurants and there are still a lot of council estates.'

There were murmurs of sympathetic assent at both her plight and Bray's. A younger woman chipped in.

'Where I am is very nice. Some people say it's working class. But it's not, it's just not.'

A slight hint of protesting too much accompanied that final statement. The older woman sought to calm things by bringing someone else into the conversation.

'Where are you living?'

'Kimmage.'

'Oh ... oh.'

Silence reigned for a few seconds before she recovered her composure.

'They say there's a real community vibe there.'

Number two returned to the conversation.

'It's a bit near Dolphin's Barn and places like that, isn't it?'

Things continued in this vein all the way to Dublin where I would round off the championship the next day at the camogie final. House prices, new builds, surveyors' reports, extensions, good areas, bad areas. This culture was more alien to me than any of the others I'd encountered that summer. But why pass judgement? These people had their own ways and I'm sure if you sat down and talked to them they'd seem perfectly normal. Live and let live, I say.

Saturday night's movie in Cineworld was not Bollywood but Mollywood, from the Malayalam cinema of Kerala, home state of the hymn-singing Jacobite Syriac congregation of Rathmines. *Devadoothan* belonged to that most common of genres, the horror musical. SPOILER ALERT: It's about a musician who becomes obsessed by an instrument which plays by itself and eventually discovers it's being played by the soul of a blind musician whose lover's father buried him alive after setting a pack of dogs on him. His spirit is haunting the mansion where it happened, which probably doesn't do much for the property value even if the mansion doesn't seem particularly working class. There are also lush romantic ballads.

Leaving the cinema I felt a tap on my shoulder and looked round to see a young Indian woman and her friend.

'Do you mind me asking why you picked this film?'

'I like Indian cinema.'

'It's unusual. Most Irish people are not interested.'

I explained how during my time in London I'd written a weekly column about Irish soccer players in England for the *Irish Post* newspaper whose office was in Southall, an area known as Little India due to the number of South Asian immigrants who lived there. Walking through Southall was an eye-opening experience for a young man fresh from the west of Ireland – the people, the clothes, the shops, the music all made it feel as though you'd temporarily warped to the subcontinent. So did the posters and the videos of the Bollywood cinema, something I hadn't even known existed up to then. The interest I developed then stuck with me and has actually grown in recent years, the massive energy, flamboyance and joy of the movies speaking to me more these days than the grim Scandinavian movies I'd once favoured. They seemed happy with the explanation.

'I'm Lakshmi,' she said, 'and this is Arjuna.'

'Lakshmi like the goddess.'

'You know a lot about India.'

'I don't know much at all but I love the movies.'

About to go, she turned back.

'That wasn't a new movie. It's a re-release from 2000.'

Just so I knew. Another formidable woman in a summer full of them.

It wasn't just Indian movies. Over the years I'd amassed a large library of DVDs and the odd Blu-ray from all over the world. I may even have started buying them around the time the ability to travel deserted me. Perhaps they became a substitute for the world I wasn't seeing. Movies gave you a look at life elsewhere in a way that books didn't seem to do. Books came to you, unless you were multilingual, as translations. There was a barrier between you and the original version. Movie dialogue was also translated but you got to hear the sound of the original language. And dialogue is only one part of movies. You got to see the texture of everyday life, the pattern of the streets, the look of the countryside, how people moved through them, the objects in their lives, a sense of what it might be like to inhabit those spaces and just as importantly how they represented their world, their thoughts and those objects. All stories may be similar at root but they're told differently in different places.

I suppose there are about 1,500 films there by now, which sounds a lot but works out at about one a week since I've been buying them. There are movies there from seventy-four different countries. It's the Ballyhaunis school of film libraries. It's not really a collection, a word which conjures up images of systematic purchase and things being carefully kept in their original boxes with an eye to future value. The remorseless march of streaming means few things have less long-term monetary worth than a stack of old DVDs. Yet they've been an invaluable investment all the same, enrapturing me, fascinating me, overjoying me, making me laugh and cry and wonder and think, getting me through bad nights and keeping a window open for me on a wider world I feared I might never see again.

Originally I sourced them from the great arthouse DVD labels, Criterion, Artificial Eye, Gaumont, BFI, Tartan, Second Run, but over the years I've also found films which haven't received English-language releases in this part of the world. eBay has brought films to me all the way from Brazil, from India, from China. There's a guy in Ostrava who sells me Czech movies in paper sleeves with English subtitles and sends me a Christmas card every year. There's a vendor in France who does a great line in obscure Japanese masterpieces and responds to specific queries as though we were engaged in espionage.

There were lots of movies from the big guns, Hollywood, France, Japan, Italy, but the gems from the margins were the ones I treasured most. My life would have been a lot poorer without the stories of two African brothers searching for their father (*Abouna*, from Chad), a bunch of friends trying to persuade a dictatorship to let them reopen a long-shut cinema (*Talking About Trees*, Sudan), a young boy in a mountain village trying to return a lost copybook so his friend won't be thrown out of school (*Where Is the Friend's House?*, Iran), an epic cattle trek from Anatolia to Istanbul by a troubled clan (*Suru*, Turkey), an awkward woman's attempts to maintain a relationship with her awkward son (*The Long Farewell*, Ukraine). All that human stuff we try to make the best of. Movies were the other great passion of my life along with sport and I'd never written a word about them. Anxiety was my guilty secret and they were my innocent secret.

There was a final lunch in the Moore Street Mall before the final walk to Croke Park. I'd inadvertently saved the best till last. The woman in the Bolivian restaurant with its half-dozen tables closely set together asked, 'Have you eaten Bolivian food before?' and explained everything on the menu with missionary zeal. There were posters of Cochabamba and La Paz on the wall and Latin music playing. I was just thinking, *Ah, the authentic folk music of the people of Bolivia*, when the song ended and the Macarena came on. My sole knowledge of Bolivia consisted of the fact that La Paz was at high altitude, something usually mentioned when Brazil or Argentina had to play there in the World Cup qualifiers.

The woman exclaimed, 'I hope you like it,' with distinct fervour as she put my chicharrón in front of me. It was one of the biggest plates of grub I'd seen in my life. There was a heap of meaty ribs, potatoes, plantain (a kind of cooked banana), a load of white corn (sweetcorn's paler and bigger cousin) and a few lumps of fat thrown in for good measure. It was food to set you up for a day tin mining in the mountains. It was delicious and after finishing it I didn't need to eat again that day. I noticed that everyone else there, a young couple, a family, a father and son, was eating even bigger plates of food and that, unlike myself, there was hardly a pick on them.

I'd asked the waitress what she'd drink to go with the meal. She recommended mocochinchi and I drank three big glasses of it. Where had this been hiding? Sundried peaches boiled in water with cinnamon and sugar and one peach left in the bottom of the glass. Bolivian food, Indian movies, Brazilian music, Munster hurling, what more could you want? The service was so friendly it felt like I'd been invited into someone's house for a meal. 'We'll see you again,' they said, and they did. I was in for more mocochinchi the next morning and with my daughter for more chicharrón when we came up for the college football game between Georgia Tech and Florida State.

There aren't many Bolivians in Ireland. A brief influx in 2023 was quickly clamped down on. So running a Bolivian restaurant seemed a quixotic venture. The Bolivians were historical underdogs; it was traditionally the poorest country in South America and had the second-highest percentage of indigenous people in Latin America, after Guatemala. Yet here they were underground in Moore Street gathering for lunch on Sunday. Things like this are a wonder.

28

The Last Waltz

CAMOGIE RODE TO THE RESCUE AND SENT THE
championship out on a high note. The football final had been
poor and the ladies' football final utterly one-sided with the
disappointing attendance adding to the feel-bad factor. The
season was ending not with a bang but with a whimper. I'd
had some good times in the previous couple of weeks, just not
inside Croke Park.

With Cork having beaten Galway by eleven points earlier in
the championship, an anti-climactic finale looked on the cards.
Instead good old underappreciated camogie produced a final
that had everything, including another terrible and possibly
decisive refereeing decision.

I took a last walk of the season to Croke Park, up the side of

Parnell Square, turning right, past Fibber Magees, Barry's Hotel, the Dergvale, crossing the road at Mountjoy Square Park, the stadium coming into sight – an experience still as thrilling to me as the first sight of the Manhattan skyline when you come in from Kennedy – down the hill opposite Fitzgibbon Court, past the barber's where, the previous week finding myself with time on my hands, I'd had a hot-towel shave and listened to the street talk of the Gael going on behind my head as I leant back in the chair, across the North Circular Road, past the crowd outside Gill's, through the barriers, along Jones' Road, another right to the turnstiles and in, up the steps and in to my seat next to five young women about the age of my eldest daughter, four in cowboy hats, one in a bucket hat, who sang the national anthem with the uninhibited freedom that came from knowing that this was their day.

Cork went two up, Galway levelled in the sixth minute. 0–3 all in the tenth. 0–4 all in the thirteenth, 0–5 apiece in the nineteenth and so on throughout a first half during which they were level eight times. Someone would score a really good point, Aoife Donohue landing a shot from long range for Galway, Orlaith Cahalane racing through for one on the run for Cork, and the response wouldn't be long in coming. They were spurring on the way sometimes jazz musicians do, the saxophonist responding to what the trumpeter is doing and vice versa as they cajole and goad each other to new heights. It was stirring stuff. Right on the stroke of half-time Galway's

Donohue put her side back ahead once more with a shot which dropped on the roof of the net.

It was 0–10 to 0–9 at half-time, which had also been the full-time score in the 2017 final won by Cork against Kilkenny. That game would have ranked as a nadir for camogie had the following year's decider, won 0–14 to 0–13 by Cork against Kilkenny, not been just as dull.

The fault was not in camogie's stars but in its rules. The referees seemed to have a horror of physical contact unsuited to an era when players were getting faster, fitter and stronger. What the Americans call ticky-tack fouls were constantly given and stalled the momentum of the game. One player who'd been vocal about the need for change was Ashling Thompson. It was a notable intervention because Thompson had been on the winning Cork teams in 2017 and 2018.

Players rarely find anything wrong with the game when they're winning but Thompson was no ordinary player. Her ferociously competitive attitude, her athleticism and her spectacular tattoos, which pre-dated the body art explosion that made Liberty Square in Thurles on a warm Sunday look like the landing of a Russian prison, made her the opposite of the comely maiden archetype once associated with camogie. Anachronistic notions about women's sport still seemed apparent in the Camogie Association's refusal earlier that year to allow players to wear shorts instead of the shorts/skirt hybrid known as skorts. The players wore shorts in training and they wore them in challenge matches but weren't allowed wear them in competitive games. It seemed not just old-fashioned but mean-spirited, especially when ladies' football imposed no such dress code.

Thompson gave the impression of chafing against the confines of the game she played, of trying perhaps to burst out of camogie and turn it simply into hurling played by women. Athletic, physically strong and a prodigiously long striker of the ball, she was a new model of camogie player. She'd spoken about struggling with depression and sometimes the way she played suggested someone not easily satisfied and striving for something just beyond her reach. It was as though Thompson's style, like her tattoos, was a declaration of freedom. The anarchist spirit burned bright within her.

Her entreaties and those of others had borne fruit – refs had lightened up and the finals got a lot better with Galway's wins over Kilkenny in 2019 and Cork in 2021 particularly enthralling. Camogie seemed to be on the road to realising its potential, and perhaps the closer it got to hurling, the bigger the chance it had of doing so.

The man beside me appeared to be Thompson's number one fan. Every one of her contributions was greeted by a bellow of 'Come on, Ashling, you're some woman for one woman.'

He was obviously a big supporter of the team, able to tell me that this player would need to improve on her semi-final showing, making reference to performances from the group stages and the league. I'd have put him at around my age but he'd been hard used. His nose was an empurpled ruin which would have given a plastic surgeon nightmares, and there was a ferocious bang of whiskey off him. Not as though he'd been drinking it but as if someone had poured a couple of bottles over him as a prelude to setting him on fire. I saw in him the road not taken, or to be more correct, the road embarked upon but turned back from.

Thompson was thirty-four now but still brooked no resistance at midfield. Galway had competed well with her in the first half but she began to take over at the start of the second. Three minutes in she struck a point to put Cork ahead after Orlaith Cahalane, grand-daughter of the Castlehaven legend Ned Cleary, had levelled. Her performance must have gladdened the heart of the clan I knew would be gathered in Croke Park.

Five minutes later Thompson got on the ball again and sent a long pass down the left wing to Amy O'Connor. There are a handful of players who send a ripple of excitement through the crowd not just when they get the ball but even when it's played in their direction. David Clifford is one, Amy O'Connor is another. In the previous year's final against Waterford she'd hit three goals in three minutes and ended up with 3–7. Often the smallest player on the pitch, she was not just a remarkable finisher but a remarkable character.

O'Connor came from Knocknaheeny on the north side

of Cork city, one of Ireland's most deprived areas. A 2014 survey found that only 4.7 per cent of the population had university degrees. O'Connor's ambitions to study pharmacy at UCC initially seemed stymied by the fact that her local secondary school didn't offer chemistry as a Leaving Cert subject. She badgered them into changing their minds, got into UCC, earned a master's in pharmacy and now worked as a project manager with a software company. She was also an evangelist for her home turf, constantly declaring her pride in coming from Knocknaheeny and staying with her local club, St Vincent's, even when it was suggested that a move to a bigger city outfit might improve her chances of making it at inter-county level.

Her fervour extended to the game of camogie itself. As a teenager she'd played on the Irish soccer team which reached the under-19 European Championship semi-finals by beating England, Spain and Sweden. Her team-mates included Katie McCabe and Megan Connolly who'd starred for Ireland in the 2023 World Cup finals and several others who went on to play professionally, but it was a route O'Connor had never considered.

'Camogie is genuinely the thing that gives me most joy in my life,' she said. Happy was the sport with a hero like this.

Galway corner-back Dervla Higgins did superbly on O'Connor, who'd actually end up scoreless from play, but this time the Cork woman got to the ball a couple of yards ahead of her, left her for dead with a sidestep, headed for goal with two backs in hot pursuit, drew another defender and handpassed to Katrina Mackey who put the ball into the net.

There was a problem. Mackey rounded goalkeeper Sarah Healy, but as she was preparing to shoot, a Galway defender got back and bumped into her. The jostle made the ball fly out of Mackey's hand and it rolled into the net without having been struck with the hurl. Cork's full-forward had effectively thrown the ball into the net. It was by accident and she hadn't been trying to hoodwink the ref but the goal was illegal all the same. Referee Liz Dempsey let it stand and that goal would divide the two teams at the end of the game.

To let one All-Ireland final be decided by a blatantly incorrect refereeing decision may be regarded as a misfortune, to let two looks like carelessness. Yet again there were attempts to minimise the importance of the call. Dempsey herself apparently tried to justify it by saying that if the goal hadn't been given she'd have awarded a penalty for a foul on Mackey. This was neither here nor there. The latitude allowed to refs in applying the advantage rule didn't extend to allowing illegal goals. As Galway manager Cathal Murray pointed out afterwards, there was no guarantee that Cork would have scored a goal from the penalty.

I suspected the ref might have missed Mackey's failure to make contact with the hurl which only became clear on close scrutiny of the action replay. To observe that Dempsey didn't have the luxury of such scrutiny was to raise the question of why she didn't. The technology was there to provide for immediate rectification of such glaring mistakes. Two whoppers in three weeks made a strong case for the introduction of a VAR system in big championship matches.

Those against such a measure liked to bring up the Premier League's VAR and the way it drove crowds to distraction when backroom officials held up play for minutes as they drew virtual lines, allowing or disallowing goals by virtue of margins as small as the edge of a boot. But a VAR system did not have to be used in the same way as the Premier League's. It could be limited to putting right the most obvious mistakes, mistakes like the free Cork hadn't been given in the hurling final and the goal they had been given in the camogie decider. They were easily spotted and the mistakes could have been almost immediately corrected. Claims that VAR was anathema to the fluid nature of Gaelic games were rendered nonsensical by the fact that games were already held up for the Hawkeye system to check whether borderline points had flown inside or outside the post. Those brief displays hadn't caused the game to collapse and a judiciously applied VAR system wouldn't either.

I'd been accused of bias for bringing up the first mistake but there was no team I wanted to win a game all year more than I wanted Cork to win that camogie final. I'd sat beside Orlaith's brother Damien and shared cans with him on the bus down from a county final. I'd stayed in her brother Dinny's house that night with the Andy Scannell Cup parked on the kitchen table. Her father Niall had offered me the keys to his house in Castletownshend at one stage when I'd been between places to lay my hat. And she was Ned Cleary's grand-daughter. I wanted her, and her sister Méabh who came on as a sub, to win the final for the sake of all those people. But you cannot not know what you do know. Bias isn't calling what you see, it's not calling it or pretending it doesn't matter. Though, given our national belief in other people's infinite deviousness, there were probably Clare fans out there who thought I mentioned the camogie final mistake to retrospectively justify making a fuss over the hurling final error.

This mistake might not have affected the result. This time the wronged team did have plenty of time to get back in the game. Though of course it was a different game to the one it would have been had the right call been made. The result might not have been affected but we can't be sure. In a game as big as an All-Ireland final we should be as sure as possible.

When Cork added a couple of points they were six up with twenty minutes left and the anticipated cakewalk looked on the cards after all. What followed instead was one of the most exhilarating interludes of the season as Galway reeled off six unanswered points in the next ten minutes. The last two came from Aoife Donohue who'd end up giving one of the great Croke Park performances in a losing cause.

It didn't look like a losing cause at the time but, with the momentum overwhelmingly behind them, Galway suddenly stalled. I'd witnessed this odd phenomenon before. A team mounts a great comeback and after drawing level finds the point which will put them in the lead much more difficult to land than the ones which put them back into the game. It's almost as though a collective sigh of relief at equalising drains the intensity which got them there. Had Galway gone a point ahead, they'd probably have won but the next five minutes were scoreless. There was a nervous 'next score wins' feel to it.

A few minutes after scoring her goal, Katrina Mackey had gone off injured and been replaced by Sorcha McCartan. The red-nosed man beside me sang McCartan's praises and said they'd be even better with her in the team. There'd been no opportunity to test his thesis because Galway had owned the ball since she'd come on.

Now with six minutes of normal time left McCartan put Cork back in the lead with a great point. Thirty years previously, her father Gregory and Orlaith Cahalane's father Niall had locked horns in the All-Ireland semi-final. Now their daughters were united in common cause, Sorcha having transferred from Down to Cork when she moved to study there. A minute later Cork were two points up and though there would be six minutes of injury-time you sensed that Galway's window of opportunity had closed. McCartan iced the cake with another point in that injury-time. Cork had won a great final and they'd won it in front of 27,811 spectators, which meant the last two deciders had been attended by the biggest camogie final crowds ever (excepting those double billed with hurling matches). Galway had endured perhaps the most disappointing three-week spell in GAA history with three successive final defeats even if the camogie team had restored some of the county's honour with their second-half rally.

Out of the stadium, down Jones' Road, across the North Circular Road, up the hill opposite Fitzgibbon Court. The jovial old boy who distributed photocopied sheets of GAA historical information was there again; the lad with the bottles of water had taken a day off. Across the road at Mountjoy Square Park, past the Dergvale, Barry's and Fibber McGees, the right turn and the descent from Parnell Square to O'Connell Street. I'd gotten into a chat with a Kerry woman living in Galway who'd seen her adopted county lose all three finals. I said goodbye at the traffic lights, darted across the road past the Ambassador and headed down Parnell Street, leaving the championship summer behind me.

On its very first day, en route to see Cork play Limerick in the football at Páirc Uí Chaoimh, I'd been hit by a huge surge of panic just after getting off the bus from Skibb. What was I doing this for? I'd never last the course, it would all go disastrously wrong somewhere along the way, better just to go home and forget about it.

I'd ducked into a café, ordered a cup of tea and a pastry and tried to get a grip on myself. I didn't have to think about the whole journey that lay in front of me; all I had to do was, as all managers advised, take each game as it comes and see how far I'd get. I finished the tea, paid my bill and set out for Páirc Uí Chaoimh. By the time I'd turned on to the long, straight road towards the ground, I was feeling a bit better. So I kept walking.

I walked out to Páirc Uí Chaoimh that day and to O'Moore Park in Portlaoise the week after. I walked in the shadow of the mountains overlooking Killarney, through a heaving Liberty Square in Thurles, from the Salthill seafront up to Pearse Stadium, out the Ennis Road to the Gaelic Grounds in Limerick, in the Athlone Road to Hyde Park in Roscommon. With every step I felt stronger.

When I got to Dublin I walked some more. I walked up O'Connell Street on my way to Croke Park, I walked down the elevator into the Moore Street Mall, to the Romanian Orthodox service in leafy Leeson Park, to the Russian Orthodox service in Harold's Cross, to the mosque on the

South Circular. I walked along the canal bank and through the bedsit land of my memory in Rathmines. I walked into my past and towards my future.

The more I walked, the stronger I felt. And when I finished walking I was a different man from the one who'd set out. I'd been the prisoner of my anxiety for so long that I'd given up believing things could ever be any different. But I'd discovered that it's never too late for change, even if you've been stuck in the same rut for decades. You just take the first step and then the next and keep going the best you can.

Along the way, you ponder a question but a clear answer always seems to elude you: What caused the attacks in the first place?

The truth is, I don't know and I probably never will. I'd been a hard drinker but all the people I'd drunk with were able to hop on planes and go on holidays. None of them were quailing at the thought of getting the bus to Cork. Getting sober some years ago had no effect on the problem. I heard exercise was a panacea so I lost five stone in six months at one stage and ran six miles four days a week. That didn't help either.

Counsellors sought to locate the origin of the attacks in some past trauma. But I had a happy childhood and nothing particularly terrible has happened to me since. I like my job, I love my kids and many things give me joy. The most bewildering and frightening thing about the panic attacks is that they seemed independent of my general state of mind. Whether I was happy or sad, relaxed or stressed made no difference.

Maybe the explanation is that there is no explanation. One drawback of telling people you've got a mental health problem is that it turns some of them into amateur psychologists. They have a theory they want to share with you or an explanation they think you should consider. Nothing could be less helpful. Every loose end doesn't need to be tied up with a neat explanation.

Montaigne, the sixteenth-century French essayist, might be the wisest writer who ever lived. Pondering why he and his best friend were so close, he concluded, 'If you press me to say why I loved him, I can say no more than because he was he, and I was I.' That's how it is. Some of us are just wired differently. You can drive yourself daft wondering why. But knowing the cause of your anxiety is ultimately less important than finding a way to cope with it. Sometimes you've just got to let the mystery be. We're not fictional characters, we're real people. We don't have to make perfect sense. We just have to live.

One walk remained. The morning after the final match I went up O'Connell Street and into Parnell Square again, but instead of turning right for the road to Croke Park kept straight on past Findlater's Church and headed north for Phibsboro. In a café round the corner from Mountjoy Prison and Dalymount Park sat The Determined Editor. She was the one who'd set the ball rolling but she'd probably expected a very different kind of book.

'Well,' she said. 'How did you get on?'

I paused for a few seconds because there were so many things I'd never said before, so many secrets I'd kept.

It was hard to know where to begin.

Acknowledgements

Thanks to Hachette Ireland for giving me the opportunity to write this book and to Claire Pelly, Aonghus Meaney and Stephen Riordan for their work.

A special thanks to my publisher and editor Ciara Considine whose hard work, assistance and encouragement were extraordinary. She ensured that it was the best book it could possibly be. I'm enormously grateful to her.

I've been lucky in my editors. John Greene of the *Sunday Independent* has been a stalwart and inspirational presence in my working life for two decades. I'm hugely thankful to him and Fergus McDonnell for putting up with my flaws and foibles for so long. Shane Scanlon of the *Irish Independent* has also been a joy to deal with. Thanks to Independent News and Media for years of loyalty, support and editorial freedom.

Thank you to my cousin Máiréad for giving me the opportunity to speak at my uncle Páraic's funeral. I hope I've done him justice. In memory of all departed members of the Feeney and Sweeney clans, in particular Páraic and Ned Feeney.

I owe my mother a debt which goes far beyond words. This book is, among other things, an effort at tribute to her indomitable spirit. My sister Maura has been a paragon of support to me through good times and bad.

To my daughters Emily, Lara and Isabel with whom I have shared the best times of my life and who have taught me a lot along the way. Every day you make me feel like the luckiest man in the world.

To their mother Siobhan Cadogan who has kept the show on the road for us all.

To everyone I encountered along the way last summer. No-one I met treated me with anything other than friendliness and kindness. There are an awful lot of nice people out there.

To Andy Whelton and Castlehaven GAA club for permission to use the pitch for the cover shot and to Ann Minihan for taking the photograph. To Castlehaven just for being Castlehaven. There can be no higher praise.

And to the GAA which might not always be perfect but remains the best thing about Ireland.

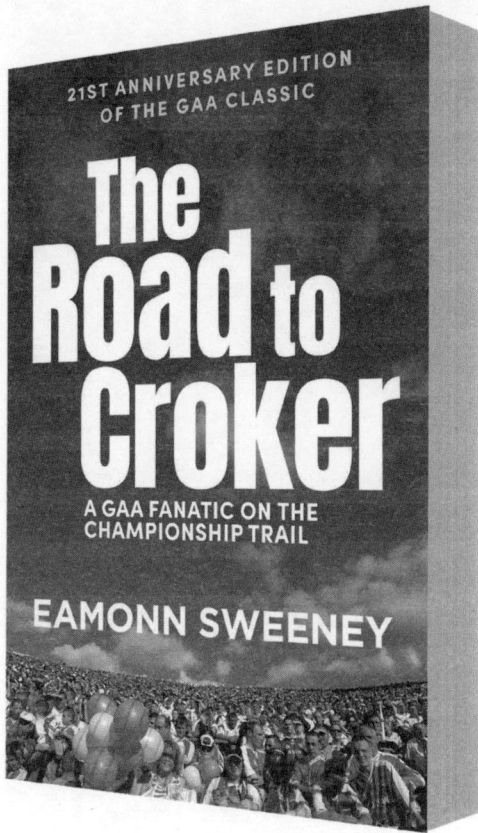